Killer B's & Worker B's

Survive or Thrive?

by Alan Hedman, Ph.D.

Overview...

Is there more to life than just surviving? Is life getting in the way of us living out our passion or dream? *Killer B's & Worker B's--Survive or Thrive?* offers us the opportunity to see how the tyranny of Killer 'B' beliefs and behaviors keeps us focused on immediate, urgent, pressing matters which prevent us from thriving — living our dream.

Alan Hedman combines his expertise in the science of thriving with extensive first hand experience working with nonprofits, educational organizations and CEOs to present a book that can help us thrive in all aspects of our lives. Living life is not the same as living life well, and Killer 'B's are the main source of the problem. These predominately good forces allow us to survive while destroying the possibility of living our dream. The result, in the words of Henry David Thoreau, is that "most people live lives of quiet desperation and go to the grave with the song still in them."

Hedman guides us through the process of identifying and neutralizing the Killer 'B's. If we have fuzzy priorities, are "nice" and selfless, are consumed by "making a living," or don't believe that we are truly 'A' material, Killer 'B's will be waiting to fill the void of our unmet dreams. Fighting with Killer 'B's is not child's play, since they can appear as subtle slayers or instant fear producers. The trick is to stay on course and take action. With the battle plans drawn on how to deal with Killer 'B's, Hedman leads us through the habits that make living a Thriving 'A' life possible.

The concepts presented throughout the book are designed to be meaningful and to provide a framework for changing our lives. A workbook and discovery guide is offered to help us begin the journey toward Thriving. At the same time, Hedman combines his sense of humor with an abundance of personal stories and examples to make Killer B's & Worker B's a fun read.

Published in the United States by TwoSixty Productions
(www.260productions.com).

ISBN: 978-0-615-32990-1

Printed in the United States of America

Designed and Produced by Rob Banning

First Edition

SPECIAL THANKS TO:

bp: Several years ago, Bruce Peltier invited me to write a chapter in his acclaimed book, *The Psychology of Executive Coaching, Theory and Practice*. I squealed but did it anyway. AND, I enjoyed the process. This inspired me to write my own book.

Couz' Dave: My cousin, Dave Siebels, made me write this book. After challenging him to implement an 'A' music project (which he did), he pointedly told me I had to write a book on *Killer* 'B's, and this is the result.

ROB: The designer and producer of *Killer* 'B's, Rob Banning, critiqued, inspired and motivated me every step of the way. He is responsible for the look and feel of the book, which was of prime importance to me.

Madison Z: In her own right, Madison Zeller is a gifted and creative writer and editor. She spent endless hours reworking my often clumsy and awkward syntax into something significantly more fun and readable. She also provided important contributions to the illustrations throughout the book.

CONTENTS

Section Five: Workbook & Discovery Guide

Section One
Warm - Up

Understanding Your Choices

In order to thrive we have to leave the hive.

Alan Hedman

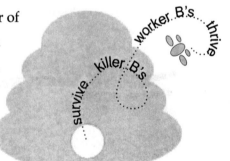

Barry Benson (voice by Jerry Seinfeld), star of the "**Bee Movie**," had just graduated from college and had an important life decision to make: would he follow the path of his father and become a HONEY STIRRER at Honex, or would he pursue the life of a swashbuckling POLLEN JOCK?!

Barry wanted to be a POLLEN JOCK; when he was presented with the possibility he realized that he was "scared out of his shorts" but knew that he must "fly outside the hive in order to be a POLLEN JOCK."

When it comes down to how we (humans) choose to live our lives, we basically have the same choices as Barry Benson:

- ≈ We can **Survive** – Live a 'B' life (WORKER 'B')

- ≈ We can **Thrive** – Live an 'A' life (THRIVER)

In brief,

- ≈ To **Survive** involves: being a good solid citizen, hard-working and diligent, living life day-to-day, reacting to whatever life presents.

- ≈ To **Thrive** means living life to the fullest, living out one's dreams, proactively living a life that matters.

Using aquatic imagery,

- ≈ To **Survive** = Floating or Dog Paddling (creating no waves)

- ≈ To **Thrive** = Swimming (making waves)

> *"Most people live lives of quiet desperation and go to the grave with the song still in them."*
> Henry David Thoreau

From this brief description of the two basic life choices, who wouldn't choose **To Thrive**?! But as Thoreau observed many years ago, most people go to the grave with the song still in them. That is, most people are merely **Surviving**, i.e. living life as a WORKER 'B'.

Some time ago an important study was conducted on 80+ year-olds to assess their perceived satisfaction with life. Among a subset of those who stated that overall they were "satisfied with their lives," close to 50% had a dream of doing something special that they didn't follow because it felt too scary and difficult. BUT, knowing what they knew about themselves at 80 years old, they realized they could have successfully implemented their dream. Instead, they would "go to the grave with the song still in them."

So, what is the problem? Why aren't more people THRIVING?

Here's the crux of the issue:

WORKER B'S ARE HIGHLY SUSCEPTIBLE TO KILLER B'S

WARNING: If you are one of those people who insist on taking things literally, what follows will make little or no sense. For example, in real life Worker Bees are the females in the hive who do all the work. The male bee (drone) does absolutely nothing except mate with the queen! In our story, WORKER 'B's are the hard-working, salt of the earth type people, male or female.

Also, in real life Killer Bees are Africanized honeybees, who bear the "killer" label for their fierce defensive action around the hive. [At this point in our story I thought it would be cool to show you pictures of real Worker Bees and Killer Bees. But in the photos I obtained, it was impossible with the naked eye to see the difference between Africanized honeybees and regular honeybees. So I didn't see the point!]

"The enemy of the best is not the bad but the good."
Goethe

Furthermore, for our story KILLER 'B's aren't even living creatures, bees or human. Rather, they are the attributes within ourselves (attitudes, behaviors, habits) that prevent us from becoming a THRIVER.

IMPORTANT REMINDER: To be a WORKER 'B' is to live a good, decent life. B's are truly "the salt of the earth."

That is to say, my kind of people! — hard-working, diligent, reliable, humble, neither selfish nor arrogant and not seeking fame or fortune. Good qualities — regular Boy Scouts and Girl Scouts! Basically, they do a lot of what is good, the very KILLER 'B' behavior which prevents them from living a THRIVING 'A' life.

The difference between survivors and thrivers

"Just because you're a WORKER 'B' doesn't mean you have to settle for 'B' activities."
Madison Zeller, Peer Counselor at Flintridge Prep.

Both THRIVING 'A's and WORKER 'B's work hard; one significant difference between the two is that THRIVERS are focused on one or two priorities while WORKER 'B's have numerous priorities. And as one expert put it, "to have 15 priorities is really to have none." It is this "scatter gun" approach that prevents 'B's from achieving 'A's.

- ≈ 'B's are a shotgun (good for lots of little game)
- ≈ 'A's are a rifle (good fo bringing down big game)

To give you a clear overview and understanding of the main ideas throughout our story, the following glossary should help.

Key Players / Key Principles

The following is offered to give you a better understanding of some of the key terms that will be used throughout our story. It is a glossary of Key Players and Key Principles.

Thrivers   **Individuals** living an 'A' life – living life to the fullest, living out their dreams.

"Life is either a daring adventure or it is nothing." Helen Keller

'A' Activities   **Habits** that make living a *THRIVING* 'A' life possible.

"We are what we repeatedly do. Excellence, then, is not an act, but a habit." Aristotle

Worker 'B's   **Individuals** who are surviving/living day-to-day, taking care of basics but not realizing or living out their dreams.

"Most people live lives of quiet desperation." Henry David Thoreau

Killer 'B's   **Attributes** (attitudes, behaviors, habits) that keep individuals focused on immediate, urgent, pressing matters. These predominately good behaviors are the most powerful force preventing us from living our dreams.

"The enemy of the best is not the bad, but the good." Goethe

'A's Trump 'B's   **Living** an 'A' life is the best way to neutralize the power of KILLER 'B's. It's easier to say "no!" [to KILLER 'B' behavior] when there's a deeper "yes!" [THRIVING 'A' activities].

"The best is the enemy of the good." Voltaire

Storytelling

Stories are the way we organize most of our experience, our knowledge and our thinking. Stories are also easier to remember (than facts or data); therefore, storytelling will be a main way of presenting the key principles.

"There have been great societies that did not use the wheel, but there have been no societies that did not tell stories." Ursula K. Le Guin

Section Two
Primer on 'A's & 'B's

Thoughts from the Experts

> Nothing survives / But the way we live our lives.

Jackson Browne

This chapter is designed to get you excited about THRIVING. Numerous writers have focused on describing what it means to live a THRIVING 'A' life. Some have conducted research on human behavior to determine the attributes that contribute to a happy, vital, and meaningful life (Mihaly Csikszentmihalyi). Others, like Po Bronson, challenge us to ask ourselves the tough questions regarding "what we should do with our lives" and what we will need to do in order to answer that question. Still, others like Rabbi Harold Kushner and Leo Tolstoy see a THRIVING 'A' life as "living a life that matters." But perhaps the ultimate "expert advice" on seeking a higher purpose in life is told in the story of an ordinary seagull who becomes transcendent – Jonathan Livingston Seagull.

Each of these experts makes distinct contributions to the true meaning of the 'A' life. Here's a closer look on what each has to say.

Mihaly Csikszentmihalyi and the Meaning of Flow

Many of us first learned of the Hungarian-born Cskszentmihalyi when he wrote the groundbreaking 1990 book, *Flow: The Psychology of Optimal Experience*. Although he can be quite "researchy" in his description of the psychological basis for happiness and fulfillment, his conclusions about the 'A' life (which he refers to as **flow**) are true gems.

Flow, according to C., means being so engrossed in an activity that we are able to shut out distractions and devote our energy to the task at hand. Flow occurs when there is a balance between *high challenges* and *personal skill level*. This is not a static process – without continual challenge, boredom creeps in. Personal growth is contingent on the balance of opportunities for action and the willingness to act upon those opportunities.

Look at the map on the next page to get a better idea of what C. is talking about.

MAP OF EVERYDAY EXPERIENCE

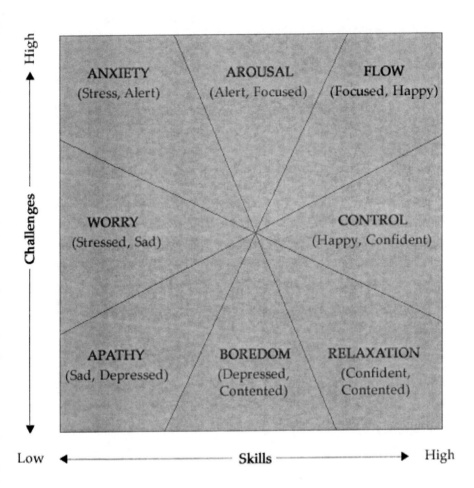

Here's what C. is trying to say! When people are taking actions that are above both their personal average level of challenges and skills, they experience **flow**. The opposite is the state of apathy, where both challenges and skills are low. When challenges outweigh skills, feelings of worry, anxiety, and arousal are produced. Or, when skills outweigh challenges, the result is control, relaxation, and boredom.

The simple conclusion: if you want to experience flow, you will need to stretch yourself both challenge-wise and skill-wise.

However, C. believes that flow by itself is not sufficient for a happy, productive and meaningful life. We must also be engaged in a worthy, ethical enterprise, working toward aspirations which we perceive as beyond ourselves and, ideally, with effects beyond our lifetime.

Although C. is obviously "pro-flow," he sees happiness as the bottom line. He says that happiness usually *follows* the fulfilling of our potential. He explains it this way:

> *"Fulfilling our potential happens when we realize that we are completely enmeshed in networks of relationships with other human beings, with cultural symbols and artifacts, and with the surrounding natural environment."*

Okay, perhaps a little dense and scholarly. But the central messages of stretching yourself, aiming high for worthy enterprises, realizing your own specialness (thank you, Mr. Rogers!), and aiming for active relationships in the world are all central to living a THRIVING 'A' life.

And now for a word from a different sort of expert, let's **flow** into the next thought.

Po Bronson on "What Should I Do With My Life?"

I consider Po Bronson an expert on THRIVING – Living an 'A' life – because he challenges us to unearth our true calling, to learn the story of our life in order to know what it's all "about." The people he interviewed for his book are ordinary people; that is, they're real. These oral histories describe how they were willing to try and answer the ultimate question of "what should I do with my life?" According to Bronson, "It's about people who've dared to be honest with themselves."

Although primarily a chronicler and social documentarian, he learned much about the path that leads people toward thriving. First and foremost, the one-size-fits all formula does not work. We are all unique (thank you again, Mr. Rogers!), therefore, each of our paths will be unique.

But that has never stopped people from wanting to believe in *the answer.* It reminds me of the great scene in the movie, *City Slickers,* where Billy Crystal and his friends almost fall off their horses to hear Jack Palance's answer to the question, "what is the meaning of life?" And how disappointed they were when he responded, "There's just *one* thing you need to know---all you have to do is find it!"

In a later section in our story the importance of "creating a crisis" will be discussed. At that time we will return to Bronson's book and share the prominent themes he learned from the people who were willing to take the challenge of living their dream.

For me, one of the most profound and inspirational experts on what it means to live an 'A' life is Rabbi Harold Kushner. Here's what he has to say.

Harold Kushner on Living a Life That Matters

Kushner's primary focus is on the human need for significance, the assurance that we matter to the world and that the world takes us seriously. He concludes that the most reliable way to matter to the world is to love the people closest to us: our mates, our children, our families, and our closest friends.

As a young rabbi he learned something very profound when he was visiting people in their last moments of life – those who had the most trouble with death were those who felt that they had never done anything worthwhile in their lives. In other words, death was not what frightened them; it was insignificance, the fear that they would die and leave no mark on the world.

"Most people are not afraid of dying; they are afraid of not having lived."

And, how to make a mark on the world? Be a good person--if you know love, have felt and given love, your life has made a difference.

But it's hard work to be a good person. Kushner uses the Biblical story of Jacob to illustrate the struggle of good and evil within us. He reminds us that only good people feel guilty; only morally sensitive people struggle with the gap between who they are and who they know they ought to be.

Jacob was acutely aware of his *yetzer ha-ra* – his evil impulses and his will to do evil. But he learned that you can't be a complete person without having to wrestle with your demons – you must be tempted or you cannot be good. And, you must be mightily tempted by your *yetzer ha-ra* in order to be capable of doing mightily good things.

Leo Tolstoy - The Death of Ivan Ilych

In Tolstoy's *The Death of Ivan Ilych*, Ivan does not realize the purposelessness of his life until he lay on his deathbed. All his life he is singularly concerned with materialistic advances; his relationships with other human beings are superficial and competitive in nature. Only as he is dying does he realize that an "A-level" life requires moral awareness and compassion for others. If you live a fulfilling life, death will leave you feeling whole rather than empty.

All of us working on living an 'A' life deal with these types of struggles. A Native American tribal leader described his own inner struggles in this way:

> *"There are two dogs inside me. One of the dogs is mean and evil. The other dog is good. The mean dog fights the good dog all the time. When asked which dog usually wins, and after a moment's reflection, he answered, "The one I feed the most."*

Now you've heard from some wise and scholarly souls on what it means to live an 'A' life. And there are so many more thinkers that could also weigh in. But what about someone simple? Someone fun. Maybe even a little corny. How about Jonathan Livingston Seagull?!

Jonathan Livingston Seagull

In 1970 Richard Bach wrote the simple story of Jonathan Livingston Seagull, a gull who wants to master the art of flying, even though his flock has told him many times that seagulls **should** concentrate solely on the process of getting food. Jonathan has tried to be a "good gull," but he cannot quell his urge to fly. Facing rejection and ridicule for his quest for greater heights, he nonetheless learns to soar and fly. He goes to a heaven-type place with other like-minded seagulls and eventually returns to Earth and helps others learn to fly. Then he vanishes and the story ends!

But the real story is that Jonathan was a seagull like all others. He was not "special" in any way. What made him different was that he chose to strive to better himself. He was not content to merely eat and sleep. He wanted to become really good at what he **could** do – fly.

Obviously this is a fable about the importance of seeking a higher purpose in life, even if your flock, tribe, family, or neighborhood finds your ambition threatening. By not compromising his higher vision, Jonathan Livingston Seagull is able to reach his ultimate goal.

But enough already of the theory and thoughts of experts (even the fun ones) on what it means to thrive. Before we can begin our 'A' journey, however, it is important to have a very clear picture on the distinction between 'A's and 'B's. That is our next task.

Distinction Between 'A's & 'B's

> Things which matter most must never be at the mercy of things which matter the least.
>
> *Goethe*

At this point, most readers are still on the path of wanting to be 'A's. They don't want to go to the grave with "the song still in their heart." Wanting to be a Pollen Jock instead of a Honey Stirrer still sounds like a good idea. And, they are inspired by the thoughts from Csikszentmihalyi, Bronson, Kushner, Tolstoy and/or Jonathan Livingston Seagull. So, what's the problem?!

For many people, two things get in the way:

1. They don't really understand the difference between 'A's and 'B's (tackled in this chapter), and;

2. They don't appreciate the power of *Killer* 'B's (the focus of the next chapter).

To truly understand the distinction between 'A's and 'B's, we begin with the work of Stephen Covey, followed by insights from Steven Sample and "Professor Joseph."

C ovey's Contribution

Stephen Covey never specifically uses the language of 'A's and 'B's in his ground-breaking books, *The 7 Habits of Highly Effective People* and *First Things First*. Nonetheless, he profoundly describes their distinction. Covey points out that we basically spend our time in one of four ways. The two main factors which define our activities are:

Urgent — things that press upon us and require immediate attention (think *Killer* 'B' behaviors)

Important — things which contribute to our high priority goals and objectives in life (think *Thriving* 'A' activities)

His time management matrix (diagrammed on the next page) helps to clarify these distinctions.

TIME MANAGEMENT MATRIX

	urgent	not urgent
important	**I** ≈ Crisis ≈ Pressing problems ≈ Deadline-driven projects ≈ Medical emergencies	**II** ≈ Preventive maintenance ≈ Relationship building ≈ Pursuing 'A' goals and opportunities
not important	**III** ≈ Some phone calls, email, voice mail, mail ≈ Some meetings, reports, "pressing" matters ≈ Popular activities	**IV** ≈ Trivia, busy work ≈ Junk mail/email ≈ Time wasters ≈ Escape activities

adapted from Stephen Covey's book *First Things First*

Quadrant I - Both Urgent and Important — Quadrant of Challenges

This is the area that requires immediate attention. These activities are usually called "crises" or "problems." We all have many Q I activities in our lives. The problem is when we are consumed by these crises.

Quadrant II - Important But Not Urgent — Quadrant of Quality

The activities in this quadrant have to do with activities like building relationships, writing a personal mission statement, long-range planning, exercising, preventive maintenance, preparation – all the important things that often get short-changed because we're too busy dealing with urgent, crisis-type activities.

This quadrant clearly defines many of the facets of 'A' activities.

Quadrant III - Urgent But Not Important — Quadrant of Deception

This is the trickiest quadrant, since we are often mesmerized by the urgency of the issues. We spend much of our time reacting to things that are urgent, assuming they are also important. But the reality is that the urgency of these matters is often based on the priorities and expectations of others.

> "Control your own time. Don't let it be done for you. If you are working off the in-box that is fed you, you are probably working on the priorities of others."
> Donald Rumsfeld

As you can see, this is the essence of KILLER 'B' behavior (much more on this in the next chapter, which deals with the power of KILLER 'B's).

Quadrant IV - Not Urgent, Not Important — Quadrant of Waste

It may be a little harsh to call this a "Quadrant of Waste," but people who feel beaten up by problems all day, every day, often choose to spend time in trivial, empty calorie-type activities. They focus on merely surviving rather than thriving.

Take a closer look at Quadrant II (the Quadrant of Quality), for this is where you will find the essence of THRIVING 'A' activity. The primary focus is on importance, not urgency. People living in Quadrant II are not problem-minded; rather, they are *opportunity-minded*. They find opportunities and starve problems. They think preventively and proactively.

These Quadrant II'ers, of course, have Quadrant I and III challenges and emergencies that require immediate attention. Although they have crises they do not live in crisis. Furthermore, the number of crises is relatively small because it is balanced by the pursuit of the 'A' goals characteristic of Quadrant II activities.

Stephen Covey remains a major influence on my thinking about 'A' and 'B' behavior, particularly on how urgency is often the culprit in preventing us from THRIVING. USC President Steven Sample, in his writings directed to organizational leaders, is also concerned with the issue of urgency and thriving.

S ample's Contribution

A practical and inspirational guide for using the Quadrant II/THRIVING 'A' activities model is described in Steven Sample's *The Contrarian's Guide to Leadership*. In this guide he proposes the Sample's 70/30 Formula--30 percent of a leader's effort should be devoted to important matters (long-range planning and goal-setting, independent thinking and inspiring his followers).

Since a leader's legacy is often determined by the long-term effects of his decisions, he suggests two "contrarian" rules to follow:

1. Never make a decision yourself that can reasonably be delegated to a lieutenant.

He suggests two compelling reasons for delegation:

> a) time constraints--leaders need to reserve energy for making important decisions

> b) delegation helps develop and nurture strong lieutenants

2. Never make a decision today that can reasonably be put off till tomorrow!

He refers to this as "artful procrastination" (as opposed to cowardly procrastination). Many times the timing of a decision can be as important as the decision--the importance of process in decision-making is often not valued as highly as it should be.

Unfortunately, there is no bright line separating substance from trivia and ephemera in decision-making. But, on balance, Sample's 70/30 Formula provides a practical upper limit on the fraction of time and effort all decision-makers should spend on important (*THRIVING* 'A') matters.

It's clear that the distinction between a *THRIVING* 'A' activity and a *WORKER* 'B' activity is often murky. Joseph's Story (below) provides some interesting insights on how to distinguish between 'A's and 'B's, which in turn can inspire taking 'A' action.

Professor Joseph's Story - A thought on how to thrive

A university professor friend recently shared a useful decision-making thought process to decipher whether a potential action is an 'A' or 'B', and how to take action on the 'A'. In brief, here was the situation he described.

Potential Action - Attend a university-wide faculty meeting, highly encouraged by his department chair.

OR

Decline attendance and work at home on a prestigious and challenging grant proposal.

Editorial Comment - It was clear that working on the proposal was the 'A' activity and going to the faculty meeting was the 'B' activity.

His Thought Process - Imagine which decision would yield the more important result. This meant looking at the predictable results AFTER the action step rather than the anticipated fears BEFORE making the decision. He knew that working on the grant proposal was more fear-provoking and challenging (a big 'A' activity clue!) than the more sedate attendance at the faculty meeting (he had been to many similar meetings!). The decision to attend this meeting would be based primarily on pleasing his boss.

His Decision - Spend three hours working on the grant proposal (attendance at the faculty meeting would also entail approximately three hours). Notify his boss of the decision. Check with a colleague to obtain highlights of the faculty meeting. In the future, he would do a monthly inventory to review 'A' and 'B' activities--retrospection is a useful way to distinguish 'A's from 'B's.

Basic Insights - 'A's can be foreboding and scary. Fear can often prevent us from taking an 'A' action step. Imagining how we will feel AFTER taking an 'A' action can be a powerful boost to prevent inaction.

It should be clear that KILLER 'B's are truly the villain in our story. To what do they owe this notoriety?! That discussion is next.

The Power of Killer 'B's

> Anything less than a conscious commitment to the important is an unconscious commitment to the unimportant.
>
> *Stephen Covey*

KILLER 'B' behavior is sneaky, subtle and seductive, conscious and unconscious, and can attack aggressively or passively. Even something as seemingly benign as neglect or complacency works just fine to keep you from becoming a THRIVING 'A' person. If you think KILLER 'B' behavior is a formidable foe, you are right! And, because KILLER 'B's often come dressed as something good, they are hard to detect.

Perhaps a visual representation will help you appreciate the difficulty in recognizing KILLER 'B' behaviors. Think of an iceberg. We usually can spot the tip of an iceberg, but most of it remains below the surface. Without the proper radar, it is impossible to detect.

KILLER 'B's often act below the surface of our conscious awareness. If we do not develop the proper detection tools, we will be like the Titanic moving through a sea of deadly hidden icebergs.

Don't forget a major tenet of this book:

WORKER 'B'S ARE HIGHLY SUSCEPTIBLE TO KILLER 'B'S

It doesn't seem fair (and who said life is fair?!), but *WORKER* 'B's are particularly vulnerable to being attacked by *KILLER* 'B's. Before you can mount any kind of offensive against *KILLER* 'B's, it is imperative to "flush them out into the open." In a moment, I will present some ways in which you can detect whether you might have problems with *KILLER* 'B's. But first, a short comedic interlude featuring Jeff Foxworthy, the "redneck comic." For no particularly good reason I've always wanted to share some of his "redneck humor" in a book!

One of his familiar stichts goes like this:

You might be a redneck **if...** (some silly examples)

≈ Your brother-in-law is your uncle AND your grandfather.

≈ You believe that beef jerky and Moon Pies are two of the major food groups.

≈ You refer to the time you won a free case of motor oil as "the day my ship came in."

You probably get the idea! In somewhat the same way, although with more serious consequences,

You might be susceptible to *KILLER* B's **if...**

You have fuzzy priorities and/or place equal importance on priority and non-priority issues in your life

The hallmark of living a *THRIVING* 'A' life is that you have a crystal clear commitment and plan for implementing the most important goals in your life. If your commitments, plans and/or goals are fuzzy, you are probably susceptible to *KILLER* 'B' behavior. Likewise, if you cannot clearly distinguish between the priority and non-priority issues in your life, *KILLER* 'B's will be happy to take over!

Example: For most of my life I have been a prime example of someone with fuzzy priorities, primarily because I placed equal importance on the numerous priorities in my life. During college it never occurred to me that some classes and assignments were "more equal than others." If a professor assigned X amount of homework, I would do X+!

One small awakening struck me in my senior year (a little late, don't you think?!) My class in Educational Methodology, comprised of massive amounts of busy work, was not as important as several other more relevant and interesting classes. With that humble jolt of awareness, I took the first small step toward developing a clarity on the importance of my priorities.

You are nice; or, you find it difficult to say <u>no</u> to requests from others, even when you want to

Killer 'B's are particularly rough on "nice people." If you are an enabler or a rescuer, Killer 'B's will find you. In order to thrive, you must be able to say no to some of the requests of others. Killer 'B's love to attack those people who will suspend their own 'A' agenda when others come calling.

Example: "Rosie" is one of the nicest people in the world. Everyone likes her and wants to be in her company, including many who are in need of rescue. When I first met Rosie, she was worn to a frazzle by all the demands she was trying to fulfill. But I soon learned that she did have an 'A' agenda, although an inability to say no to the 'B's, or the "shoulds," made attainment of the 'A's, or the "coulds," impossible. With a lot of difficult work, particularly in regulating time spent with needy people, she was better able to work on those activities that helped her Thrive.

You are living a 'B' life because "you have to make a living."

Killer 'B's are vicious with people who stuff their dreams and concentrate on the necessities of day-to-day living. Worker 'B's often do not move to 'A' activities because their lives are already filled with the requirements and responsibilities they feel are necessary to survive.

Example: My cousin Dave gave me a great insight about the mentality of many self-supporting musicians. He pointed out that most musicians will accept almost any gig that comes their way. The common motto is: "A bird in the hand is worth more than two in the bush." And, if you want to feed your family, you better take all gigs, including those that are clearly 'B's. The myth often believed is that by making yourself available, anywhere/ anytime, you will magically find the person or situation that will result in 'A' work. But in most cases if you primarily accept 'B' work, you will continue to live in a 'B' world.

> *"The urgency addiction is a self-destructive behavior that temporarily fills the void created by unmet needs."*
> Charles Hummel

You are plagued by busyness

In *The Tyranny of the Urgent*, Charles Hummel describes the urgency addiction as a "self-destructive behavior that temporarily fills the void created by unmet needs." WOW! In other words, if you are not living your dream, KILLER B's will fill the void.

Example: Many people I know believe the following motto: "Idle hands are the tool of the devil." Years ago I was reading Laura Ingalls Wilder's *Little House on the Prairie* series of books with our daughter. Story after story depicted a hard-working family that had no time for idleness.

One painfully amusing story went like this: Laura and her father were threshing wheat by hand. From previous experience they knew it would take six to eight weeks of very long days to complete the task. Laura cautiously mentioned to her father that a threshing machine could complete the task in several hours. Her father's response? "Why would we want to do that? All we would do is save time. What would we do then, sit around and twiddle our thumbs!"

I had to stop reading---the example was just too close to home! Being plagued by urgency and busyness can be an addiction that prevents us from doing our best.

Americans, by and large, are super busy. With so many "shoulds" and so many responsibilities to fulfill, they are unable to act upon their dreams on a daily basis. As Covey's opening quote suggests, most of the decision-making process to succumb to a *KILLER* 'B' is unconscious. The resulting urgent actions are often good, but they are not the best. To live your dream you must identify and understand your personal *KILLER* 'B's. Respect their power but don't let them win the battle of how you live your life.

Why So Many Worker 'B's

> Hanging on in quiet desperation is the
> English Way.
>
> *from Pink Floyd*

The previous chapter, The Power of KILLER 'B's, goes a long way toward explaining why there are so many WORKER 'B's and so few THRIVING 'A's. Even when someone has the best intentions of being an 'A,' KILLER 'B's can derail or destroy that dream. But there are other reasons that help explain the paucity of 'A's; some are obvious and conscious, while others are not so obvious and probably unconscious.

Oh, and by the way, the English do not have a corner on the market when it comes to "hanging on in quiet desperation!"

Here are what I believe to be some of the major reasons for the scarcity of 'A's:

Many people are happy being a 'B'

The most obvious reason for the preponderance of WORKER 'B's is that it is easier to be a 'B' and/or people are perfectly happy being a 'B'. No need to dig any deeper because there is nothing pathological about being a decent, honest, salt of the earth type person, content to live life day-to-day rather than searching for some greater meaning in life.

Many people settle for becoming a 'B'

Many people want to become an 'A'; they like the idea of "going for the gold" but end up settling for far less. Settling, in fact, is one of the most powerful weapons in the KILLER 'B' arsenal. The Pickle Theory, authored by Jim Douglas, describes the process of settling very well.

The Pickle Theory

You really want a pickle

For some unknown reason, you are salivating at the thought of a nice crunchy pickle!

You go to the refrigerator

But alas, there is no pickle in the fridge. Why? Maybe you were too busy with one of life's many urgent matters to actually purchase a pickle; or you just got distracted, or..............No matter how many times you open the fridge, there is no pickle. Then you are left with accepting filler — day old meatloaf, stale leftovers, or the the like, instead of your true desire — a delicious, crunchy pickle. You have succumbed to one of life's toughest and most subtle KILLER 'B's.........SETTLING.

The Pickle: any THRIVING 'A' activity

The Fridge: where and how you plan to implement your 'A' activity

The Moral: If you really want a pickle, it must be ready and available and in plain sight the next time you head for the refrigerator. Otherwise, you will have to settle for something less.

For those of you who are not into pickles, be like Arlo Guthrie in his "motorsickle song."

"I don't want a pickle, I just want to ride my motorsickle."

NOTE: The Pickle Theory is not to be confused with the more famous Pickle Jar Theory, by Jeremy Wright. The focus of his theory is how to insure that your most important priorities are tackled first. (You will get to know that theory in the section on "Implementing Your 'A's.")

t's too hard (being an 'A')

There's no getting around the fact that being an 'A' is hard work and that it requires consistent effort, very much like a farmer. I grew up with dairy farmers who milked their cows every day, twice a day, whether they felt like it or not. They also worked their fields on a regular basis. Milking cows and growing crops is not only hard work, but it also must be done on a regular, consistent basis in order to be successful.

Implementing your 'A's requires the same level of commitment as successful farming; and, sometimes it is just too hard. Milking cows, growing crops, and working your 'A's have a lot in common--long, hard and consistent work. This kind of hard work is discouraging for many, which is another reason for the scarcity of THRIVING 'A's.

The above reasons for the preponderance of WORKER 'B's are fairly obvious and involve conscious decisions. But there are other reasons that are not so obvious and that are often unconscious. What follows are two such examples.

Many don't believe they are 'A' material

"Until I believe that it is, I am believing that it is not."
Henry Ford

Many people who are really Major League material honestly think of themselves as having only Minor League ability. You don't have to know baseball to understand this description! If you really don't think of yourself as 'A' material, the case is closed--you won't become an 'A.'

Believing you are 'A' material is often difficult because of confusion between selfishness, selflessness, and self-centeredness. Let me explain! As 'A' material, you need to be willing to be selfish. To be selfish means to be someone with a clear passion and vision, willing to take the necessary steps to fulfill that dream even when others intrude with outside pressure and demands.

CAUTION: If you look up selfish and self-centered in the dictionary, they will be described in a negative context. As you can see, I am describing them in a very different and distinct way.

Dictionary Definitions:

≈ *self-centered*: thinking chiefly of oneself or one's affairs.

≈ *selfish*: acting or doing according to one's interests and needs without regard for those of others, keeping good things for oneself and not sharing.

I come from a large tribe of people who was taught that selflessness was a virtue and selfishness and self-centeredness were sinful. Imagine my horror when a psychological best-seller appeared, entitled *The Art of Selfishness*. What next, I pondered, "The Art of Serial Killing?!"

But now I see selfishness in a much different light. I once heard selfishness described as the ability to fill your own bucket so you will have something to share with others. And, that selflessness (an empty bucket) would make it impossible for you to be a loving, giving person.

If you don't love yourself, it is impossible to love others; if you don't know how to feed yourself you won't be able to feed anyone else. In other words, you need to make sure that your bucket is full; this is the "art" of selfishness.

> *"It is one of the most beautiful compensations of this life that no man can sincerely try to help another without helping himself."*
> Ralph Waldo Emerson

If you have a dream and want to "go for it," you will have to be selfish (I can hear my mother rolling over in her grave as I write this!). This is obviously a wide departure from my earlier belief training. But I still have a strong aversion for self-centeredness, which is a narcissistic view that says you really think of yourself as the center of the universe — which is not true!

If you are of a biblical persuasion or background, the story of Jesus' visit with the sisters, Mary and Martha, in the New Testament (Luke 38 - 42) might give you a new perspective on the importance of living your priorities rather than selflessly serving others. Here is the story, using The New Testament in Modern English translation by J.B. Phillips.

> Jesus came to a village and a woman called Martha welcomed him to her house. She had a sister by the name of Mary who settled down at the Lord's feet and was listening to what he said. But Martha was very worried about her elaborate preparations and she burst in, saying: "Lord, don't you mind that my sister has left me to do everything by myself? Tell her to get up and help me!"

> But the Lord answered her: "Martha, my dear, you are worried and bothered about providing so many things. Only a few things are really needed, perhaps only one. Mary has chosen the best part and you must not tear it away from her!"

Jesus' Message — He delicately rebuked Martha's choice of values; a simple meal (one dish) was sufficient for hospitality. Jesus approved and praised Mary's choice to listen to his teachings, while he disapproved Martha's choice to engage in unneeded acts of hospitality.

The Bigger Picture — If you have a dream and if you believe that you are 'A' material, your priorities need to match this vision. This may entail being selfish, letting some 'B' activities go undone, and acting as though you are

'A' material even when you are shrouded with serious doubts.

F ear of Success

> *"Failure's hard, but success is far more dangerous. If you're successful at the wrong thing, the mix of praise and money and opportunity can lock you in forever."*
> Po Bronson

Being successful can be a burden. It can mean more responsibility, more people wanting something from you and increased time in the limelight. Being an 'A' can mean acquiring one or more of these burdens. It is truly hard to be an 'A' and remain invisible.

Many people are confused on how to become successful while still being selfless and humble. Well, forget about being selfless! This simply means living off the wishes and desires of others, placing your own 'A' activities at the mercy of others.

But what about humility? Isn't that a good thing? Yes, it is. The problem for many people is that being humble means being self-deprecating, selfless and wimpy. This reminds me of a major theological question I had from many years ago. The bible says, "Blessed are the meek, for they shall inherit the earth." I felt truly on the horns of a dilemma — should I become a wimp (i.e. meek) and inherit the earth, OR be a swashbuckler and end up in hell!"

Luckily, much later in life, I learned that this was a false dilemma. The true meaning of meek is "humility with strength," not wimpiness. Why didn't someone tell me this earlier?! I now believe that it is not a contradiction to be courageous, strong and humble. My strongest praise for some-one is to refer to him/her as a "velvet hammer," which conveys someone with a courage of conviction while maintaining a well-balanced sense of strength and humility. Since humility with strength is a key ingredient for success, it is possible to be successful and still remain grounded.

There are clearly many challenges related to *KILLER* 'B's and the power they have to prevent us from living a *THRIVING* 'A' life. But, if you can believe that you are 'A' material, let go of the fear of success and be will-ing to put up with some hard work in return for great dividends--LISTEN UP!!

What follows is the only chapter where I blatantly turn into a cheerleader. Namely, **You Deserve to Be an 'A'.**

You Deserve to Be an 'A'

" Why Not the Best?

Jimmy Carter

As promised, this chapter is a blatant exercise in cheerleading, maybe even a "preachy" attempt in trying to convince you of your perfect right to be an 'A.'

Your Perfect Right

During the mid-70's (that's the mid 1970's for you younger readers!), a self-help movement was in vogue: assertion training. Numerous books were written on learning the distinction between assertiveness, non-assertiveness and aggression. The description of each behavior was defined in terms of my rights and your rights. Therefore:

Non-assertion = respecting the other person's rights but not your own;

Aggression = respecting your rights but not the rights of others; and

Assertion = respecting your rights **and** the rights of others.

The primary goal of these training programs was to help people learn techniques on how to be assertive, without being aggressive or non-assertive. Many excellent techniques were clearly described and demonstrated. But this often did not translate to new behavior — in spite of this clarity, many people were still unable to implement the assertion skills. What was the problem?

According to the astute observation of Robert Alberti, author of *Your Perfect Right,* the problem was in the belief system. It was clear, he noted, that people must believe they have the right to be assertive before they can implement the appropriate assertiveness skills.

Ditto for becoming an 'A' — first comes the belief that you deserve to be an 'A'; then comes the action.

Why Not Be Your Best?

In the 1976 presidential election, I was in a quandary on how to cast my ballot. Then I came across a book title written by one of the candidates that fascinated me — *Why Not the Best?* by Jimmy Carter. From his religious upbringing as a Southern Baptist he had been taught to be humble and "unprideful." Not wanting to be seen as boastful or arrogant had resulted in a life of good achievements, but none that were truly his best.

This changed when he was a young naval midshipman serving under the legendary Admiral Hyman Rickover. As he was inspecting a project completed by Carter, Rickover commented that he had done a good job. But Rickover challenged Carter with the admonition that he could do better. Rickover asked directly, "Why not your best?"

This so inspired the young Carter that he dedicated his life to asking himself at each future junction, "Why not the best?" He understood being an 'A' required believing that he deserved to be an 'A.'

Parable of the Talents (Matthew 25: 14-30, New Testament)

Some God-fearing people believe that to understate your talents is a good way to prevent arrogance. But this beautiful and hard-hitting story from the bible clearly illustrates what God expects from us. Here is the story:

It begins with a man who was preparing to leave home on a journey. He called his servants and distributed his property to them based on ability. To one servant he gave 5 Talents (5,000 dollars, a lot of money in those days!). To another servant the man gave 2 Talents and to a third he gave only 1 Talent. Then the man left. The servants were on their own.

As the story goes: "He who had received the 5 Talents went at once and traded with them; and he made 5 Talents more. So also, he who had the 2 Talents made 2 Talents more. But he who had received 1 Talent went and dug in the ground and hid his master's money."

Eventually, the master returned to settle accounts with his servants. He was quite pleased with the two who had taken their Talents and put them to good use. To each he said: "Well done...enter into the joy of your master." The man was not nearly as kind to the servant who had hidden his Talent in the ground, thereby making no use of it at all. Now labeled "the worthless servant," he was sent away "into the outer darkness where men will weep and gnash their teeth."

The message of this parable is clear and simple--God gives each person X amount of talents. Even though each of our talent allotment is different, the real question is what we do with the ones we have. It seems that God not only believes we deserve to be our best, but he also expects us to do so, regardless of the amount of talents we have.

The 'A' List 'A's

The list of famous 'A's is long and impressive. On this list are the many national and international heroes who have lived life to the fullest, setting high goals and relentlessly pursuing their dreams while usually facing great adversity. My personal list of such heroes includes Nelson Mandela, Helen Keller, Martin Luther King, Mohandas Gandhi, Jackie Robinson, Eleanor Roosevelt and Chief Joseph. Each of these heroes are great role models.

BUT, because they are often seen as being "bigger than life," not at all like most of us "normies," it can be difficult to identify with them. "They" may be able to accomplish great things, but what does that have to do with little 'ol me! For inspiring stories of people who are making a difference in the world, and with whom I can identify, I like to turn to human interest stories about real people. The stories below are the kind that always leave me thinking — if "they" can do it, why can't I?!

This is the power of those I call The Quiet 'A's.

The Quiet A's

Unlike the 'A' List 'A's, the "Quiet A's" do not appear to be bigger than life. They are literally our next door neighbors, no smarter or better looking than we are, and often unknown to the world until their death. But it is clear in hearing their stories that they have not gone to the grave "with the song still in them." Listen to just a few inspiring stories of ordinary people who are living extraordinary, THRIVING 'A' lives.

Joe's Story - One Life Can Make a Difference

Consider the life of Joseph Daniel McQuany (1928 - 2007), better known as "just Joe" in his home town of Little Rock, Arkansas. He touched and transformed the lives of thousands with his inspirational actions in combating drug and alcohol addiction.

The secret of his success? "If I hadn't been an alcoholic, I probably would have amounted to nothing." After getting sober in 1962, he founded a program called Serenity House, an offshoot of AA. The program became highly successful, primarily because of Joe's personal experience. To quote a co-worker who knew him well, "His soft, unjudging dark eyes would connect with the souls of others. Joe seemed to look past all the superficialities that separate us one from another, and see the essential creature within."

If an ordinary Joe like this can make a difference, what does that say to the rest of us?

"Do not sign a death warrant to your dream."
Elsie Karr Kreischer

Elsie Karr Kreischer's Story - Words of Wisdom

Elsie Karr Kreischer, 87, has been teaching spring and fall classes on how to write and sell children's picture books for nearly 22 years at the University of New Mexico's Continuing Education division. With a style best described as careening from ornery drill sergeant to supportive grandmother, she shares quotes of wisdom with her students. I know I'm a sucker for quotes, but listen to these:

"You cannot become what you want by remaining what you are!" — Kreischer's advice to her writing classes.

"If you dream of writing a book, you can. Learn the simple techniques. Dreaming is half the journey." — Kreischer's message on living your dream.

"Write with a debt of honor and make a commitment to finishing what you write. It may be like putting an octopus to bed. But do it." — Kreischer's charge to keep on keeping on, particularly when the going gets tough.

By all accounts, Kreischer is another "ordinary" person who uses dreaming, learning and persevering to live an extraordinary life.

Julia Sperring's Story - Lessons in Life

Six months after being diagnosed with cancer, Shelia Madsen got a phone call from Julia Sperring saying she'd heard that Madsen had received a dulcimer for Christmas. Being acquaintances, Sperring, 81, invited Madsen, 67, to join her dulcimer class.

"Julia has a way of making you feel you are doing a favor for her when she is actually doing something for you," says Madsen of her dulcimer teacher, who charges nothing for her classes and even loans students an instrument if they need one.

Now, every Tuesday afternoon, Madsen is one of about a dozen students, ranging in age from 10 to 80, who take lessons in a renovated hog barn on the Sperring family farm in Live Oak, Fla. (pop. 6,480). "The youngest to the oldest have found joy and healing in the music," says Madsen, who is now cancer-free. Even more special, though, are the experiences shared across generations under the watchful tutelage of Sperring, a retired telephone company worker who began playing the dulcimer at age 72.

"All this has happened because she lives every day as a celebration of life," Madsen says. "Although Sperring has just gone through her second bout of cancer, she still looks on every moment as an opportunity to do something for someone. She is a gracious, caring lady who thinks she is giving us lessons in music, but we know we are getting lessons in life."

Lessons in life, indeed. Sounds like some simple and profound lessons to learn from an "ordinary" lady living an 'A' life.

Cousin Dave's Story - The New Music Man

Cousin Dave is also a real person and is really my cousin — he insists that as the son of my first cousin he is really my cousin once removed, or something like that! But I digress. Dave is a musician, a very good musician, and has been for a very long time. Dave is also the inspiration for this book, AND he is particularly responsible for clarifying my thinking on "WORKER 'B's and KILLER 'B's". The story goes something like this:

My couz and I are renowned for lively discussions, usually ones that focus on solving most of the problems of the world! On one such momentous occasion I was talking about some new ideas I had on why so few people were truly living 'A' lives, even though they loved the concept. I told him the real problem was the KILLER 'B's, those perfectly good activities that effectively kill 'A' level living. And, that it was a particular problem for WORKER 'B's like the two of us. The usual culprits were quickly identified:

I have to make a living; I'm already too busy with commitments to start on some big A-type projects, etc. When I asked if he had an 'A' music project or dream, he quickly outlined it. Then I went on a roll — "Why don't you take a chance and go for it. Outline the plan you need to take, especially the scary phone calls and actions steps. And probably most critical of all --identify the KILLER 'B' activities you need to eliminate."

And, he agreed!

Just to keep you in suspense, I will withhold the result of his project until we hear Dave's side of the story in "Implementing Your 'A's." At this point, it is simply enough to note that he had to begin by believing that he deserved to be an 'A.' While working on his project, he got frisky and suggested (pointedly, I might add) that I should initiate my own 'A' project — writing a book on KILLER 'B's and WORKER 'B's.

And, I agreed!!

Stories can often motivate you to take action on those "songs that are in your heart." I hope you feel inspired by the real life characters I have described. The next chapter is designed to further motivate and inspire you, by outlining how doing 'A' activities can actually trump 'B' activities. Is that good news or what?!

What? A blank page?

- Plagued by busyness.
"To busy" Living your life, but not enjoying life experiences.
- The Pickle story

- Killer B's can ~~often~~ often appear as good thing and may hard to ~~detect~~.

Joseph's story — work on the thing that brought fear. ~~is~~.

'A's Trump 'B's

The best is the enemy of the good.

Voltaire

We have talked at length about the power of *KILLER* 'B's, how fear, complacency and feelings of unworthiness can prevent us from living a *THRIVING* 'A' life. We have also discussed how we are susceptible to *KILLER* 'B's if:

≈ we have fuzzy priorities in our life;

≈ we are "nice" and have difficulty saying **no** to unwanted requests from others;

≈ we are consumed by surviving, i.e., "making a living"; and/or

≈ we are plagued by busyness.

Yes, it is important to acknowledge the power of *Killer* 'B's and to be mindful that attacking them will be difficult. BUT, *Thriving* 'A' activities have some built-in qualities that allow them to "trump" *Killer* 'B' behavior. Namely,

The Passion of Vision

"It's easier to say 'no!' when there's a deeper 'yes'!"
Stephen Covey

Having a clear vision makes it possible to say "no" to those clever, subtle *Killer* 'B' behaviors which can destroy or derail a dream. And with the passion which accompanies a clear vision, you are prepared to say "yes" to your dreams.

Think of a time when you were passionate about a decision you were about to make. Could anything stop you from moving forward? Now, imagine what would happen if you made a conscious decision to choose 'A' activities on a regular basis so as to make it a habit. Clearly, you would be unstoppable.

Boldness - The Power of Starting

*"Whatever you can do, or dream you can do, begin it. **Boldness** has genius, power and magic in it."*
Goethe

As one wag put it, "the best way to start is to start." Cute and accurate, but it's probably not very motivating or inspiring. But what about this--think back to a decision you made that left you feeling really good about yourself. It was probably part of a bigger dream you had for yourself. And, you were probably scared to take action. But you did it anyway. Boldness, with its "genius, power and magic" helped you take action.

It is very easy to become stagnant. Recapturing the magic of boldness can get you back on track. Thinking bold thoughts will result in taking the first steps toward THRIVING 'A' activities. Being bold on a regular basis will make it a habit.

t's Hard to Go Back

"I've learned......that if one advances confidently in the direction of his dreams, and endeavors to live the life which he has imagined, he will meet with success unexpected in common hours."
Henry David Thoreau

When 'A' activities become a habit, it is very hard to go back to being a WORKER 'B'. After you've had a taste of the finest wine, can you go back to drinking Ripple?! What about spending quality time with a friend who truly inspires and challenges you - is it possible to return to those who drag you down? And after actively engaging in THRIVING 'A' activities, how does it feel to return to the mundane, reactive B-Level activities?

Barry Benson, our animated hero from the "Bee Movie," is a good example of someone who found it "hard to go back." In spite of much fear and trembling he became a Pollen Jock, and once a "jock," he never looked back!

Thoreau, in the above quote, describes how the unexpected successes you experience when you follow your dreams make it very difficult to return to the common life. One of my favorite "'A' list 'A's", Eleanor Roosevelt, shares how the frightened and invigorating 'A' journey, in which you look fear in the face, results in strength, courage and confidence. Who would want to return to merely surviving after living as an 'A'?!

Here is how she puts it:

> *"You gain strength, courage and confidence by every experience in which you really stop to look fear in the face. You are able to say to yourself, 'I lived this horror. I can take the next step that comes along.' You must do the thing you think you cannot do."*

'A's, because of their passion and boldness, make it difficult to go back to the status quo: 'A's truly trump 'B's. Now all we have to do is learn how to discover our 'A's and begin the steps for implementation. But first, a reminder.

REMINDER: There is nothing wrong with living a 'B' life; if you want to "be a 'B'," that's fine. If you are perfectly happy being a Honey Stirrer, there is no need to figure out how to become a Pollen Jock! **But don't settle!**

The rest of our story is for those who want to develop a master plan for living the 'A' life. In our next section, "Discovering Your 'A's," we will examine four different ways of finding that special something in order to give your life unique meaning.

More space to take notes!

Section Three
Discovering Your 'A's

Seriously Listen to Your Dreams

Nothing happens unless first a dream.

Carl Sandburg

It may surprise you to know that dreaming isn't really about sleeping; it's about waking up. Dreams, whether literal or metaphorical, can wake us up and make us realize challenges and opportunities that lie ahead. They can tell us what we need to know and alert us of actions we need to

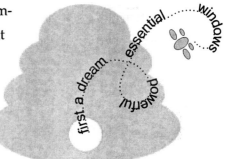

take. And, they can personally and profoundly help us recognize our 'A's. Joseph O'Neill, scientific thinker and researcher, defines it this way: "The power of dreams, like the power of myth, is that the analogies are deep and perfect."

Throughout history — from ancient shamans to the Bible to Freud and Jung — men and women from all cultures have been fascinated by dreams and pondered their meaning and power. And with the help of recent scientific research, dreams have been shown to have a real, practical function as well as a way of sparking our imaginations in unexpected ways.

A brief overview:

Dreams are essential for basic survival

Antti Revonsuo, a Finnish psychologist, theorizes that dreaming is central to human evolution. "A dream's biological function is to simulate threatening events and to rehearse threat perception and threat avoidance." That is, dreams can warn us of challenges ahead and give us a chance to rehearse effective responses.

From personal experience

An unknown author has said, "My life has been filled with a series of terrible disasters which have never occurred!"

In my case, I specialize in having nightmares (not unlike many others I know). On one particular occasion I experienced a repetitive, almost identical scary dream for three consecutive nights. It centered on a meeting scheduled with a rather intimidating administrator, who I predicted would be extremely unhappy with a recent series of decisions I'd made.

After the third night of these terrifying dreams, I finally got the "hint" that I needed to do something. The next day I proactively developed my plan of attack. First, I decided which of the decisions in question was the most important. Second, I wrote out the reasons for making the decision and what I hoped would be the desired outcome; the writing helped me clarify the main points for the discussion. Then, I visualized how I wanted to present myself to my boss (confident and open to constructive criticism) and what I wanted to say. With the opportunity to practice and rehearse my actions, the meeting was actually quite positive.

Dreams can alert us to internal dangers

They may tell us what is going on inside our bodies and what we need to do to stay healthy. Nurse Mary Agnes Twomey of Baltimore, for example, dreamed she'd traveled inside her body and found it was like a boiler room in danger of blowing up. Upon waking, she made a doctor's appointment where she learned she had an ulcer that needed treatment.

Dreams allow us to look at the world in a new way

"Dreams allow us to play and experiment with new conditions or find novel solutions," says Richard C. Wilkerson from the International Association for the Study of Dreams. "They allow us to explore unique areas of life and practice new behaviors."

Dreams can be a fertile source of creativity because they routinely make new and unexpected connections. Dr. Ernest Hartmann, a psychiatry professor at Tufts University, explains it this way: "In dreams, connections are made more easily then in waking, more broadly and loosely." And he profoundly adds, "The connections are not random. They are guided by the emotional concerns of the dreamer."

In dreams you may gain new insights about personal relationships or develop exciting new ideas. OR, you may get a crystal clear perspective on what your 'A's are and what action you need to take in order to fulfill those dreams.

Dreams can be the window to our soul

Dreams can be generated both consciously and unconsciously. Consciously we need to be continually asking ourselves questions like, "What do I want to be when I grow up? Am I really doing what I want to be doing?" But it is in the unconscious dream world where our seemingly random thought processes can lead to profound insights which boldly mobilize us to take steps toward living our dream.

To illustrate this concept, I will share one such vivid dream. I credit this dream with a major assist in rudely knocking me out of complacency into a frightening and exciting new world of risk-taking.

> *"Dreams allow us to play and experiment with new conditions."*
> Alan Hedman

Personal Dream

I was living a "good" life, with an okay job, but was continually contemplating something more meaningful, more fulfilling, and more challenging. And then one night this dream:

I'm 75 years old and had just finished working 45 years at Organization X (without having missed one day of work due to sickness, mind you!). I came back to my job site, sat down on a bench and was soon joined by another old-timer. I babbled on about how proud I was to work here, how great the job was, blah, blah, blah.

My new bench mate waited patiently for me to finish and then told me his story. He had worked in another department at this organization for about eight years but was itching to go independent. But the timing was horrible--a young family, new house, etc. However, when he approached his wife about his wild and crazy idea, she said, "Let's go for it; you only live once." For the next 25-30 years they had a series of exciting and challenging ventures throughout the world.

At that point in the dream my jaw dropped to the floor. I woke up in a cold sweat, and although petrified, I knew what I had to do. The next day I tendered my resignation with my boss, who kindly wished me the best in my "new life."

The moral of the story? When dreams, literal or metaphorical, conscious or unconscious, knock on your heart's door — **SERIOUSLY LISTEN.** They may just be providing you with a way to discover the "touchstone of your character," that profound and personal 'A' dream you have for your life.

Nope. Nothing here.

Wow I like that personal dream.
All we have to do is listen. Quiet
the mind and listen.

Make Use of Jealousy and Envy

66 Envy shoots at others and wounds itself.

Swedish Proverb

The Swedish proverb quoted above accurately captures the idea that many of us have about the meaning of *jealousy* and *envy* — namely, that they are bad emotions and need to be avoided whenever possible. Worse, it is believed, when we "shoot at others" we really end up wounding ourselves. In fact, when you check out the dictionary definitions, you will not find anything useful for "discovering your 'A's."

jealousy — feeling or showing resentment toward a person whom one thinks of as a rival.

envy — feelings of discontent aroused by someone else's possession of things one would like to have oneself.

NOTE: For a serious academic discussion on jealousy, see the summary ideas from *Psychology Today* in the addendum at the end of this chapter.

There is no question that we can get eaten up by jealousy and envy. But, I believe there can also be a very positive application of these emotions--they can truly help us discover our 'A's. Once again I have taken the liberty to define something generally considered negative (like selfishness earlier) in a positive, useful way. To better understand how this works, we need to take a short stroll down "Projection Lane."

U nderstanding Projection

"We see things not as they are, but as we are."
Unknown

Projection is a psychological term, usually credited to Freud. It says that when we experience powerful negative emotions we are more likely to put them on others (project) rather than take personal ownership. That is, we put unto others that which truly belongs to us. For example, if I call you cheap, it is probably because I'm stingy; if I see you as being power hungry, it could be because I am controlling, etc.

Projection is a powerful emotion. One of my supervisors in graduate school bluntly stated, "Projection runs the world." For a long time I did not want to believe this to be true. Now, however, I'm a 'true believer' in the deadly power of projection. And, because many people find it difficult to accept personal responsibility for their negative feelings and emotions, the notion that they are projecting often goes undetected. A good way to discover whether or not you are projecting is captured in this rhyme:

You spot it,

You got it.

This rhyme points to the mirror-like quality of projection. If you "spot" an attribute in another person you don't like, pretend that you are looking in a mirror, because you've probably "got" that same attribute.

NOTE: If you are interested in seeing how projection can be applied in a humorous way, check out the addendum at the end of this chapter.

But now, on to the positive applications of projection! Don Miguel Ruiz, author of *The Four Agreements,* has a very useful way of describing how to positively use the words and feelings others project onto us. He gives the following personal example:

"Imagine someone says, 'Miguel, what you are saying is hurting me!' But it is not what I am saying that is hurting you; it is that you have wounds that I touch by what I have said. You are hurting yourself."

As described by Ruiz, this idea of personal importance, or taking things personally, is key to how each of us can positively use negative emotions. We need to pay attention to what it means when we project these feelings on others. If we can own the feelings attached to jealousy and envy, we have the opportunity to discover and identify the very 'A' list activities we want to be doing in order to thrive. It works like this:

Jealousy Helps Us Distinguish Between Shoulds and Wants

As discussed in the earlier section on "the distinction between 'A's and 'B's," it is hard for many of us to truly feel our 'A's because we are so filled with rational *"shoulds."* It often takes the powerful jolt of jealousy to help us realize what we really want to do rather than simply what we should be doing. The *"wants"* usually represent our 'A' activities, while the *"shoulds"* are the KILLER 'B's which prevent us from moving toward our dreams.

A small but profound example helped me distinguish between my *wants* and *shoulds*: I was watching a special on Malcolm Forbes as he trium-phantly flew around the world on his private Lear jet to exotic villas. I experienced not a speck of jealousy; owning a private jet and mansions were clearly not on my personal 'A' dream list.

> *"Jealousy can stretch us in identifying our dreams and goals."*
> Alan Hedman

Jealousy Realistically Stretches Us

One of the main points about 'A's is the notion that in order to thrive, we will need to stretch ourselves. If an activity is too easy, we will be bored. If an activity is too hard, we will be scared and intimidated and probably not make an attempt.

Jealousy can show us what we truly are capable of doing and what, in fact, is realistic for us to be doing. For example, if I see someone dunking on an 8' basket, I do not get jealous because that activity is (or at least, was!) too easy. On the other hand, I am not jealous of the world-class sprinters, pole vaulters, etc. because I am not (and never was) capable of challenging them. But when someone tells me they just went on a five-day wilderness hiking and fishing trip, jealousy reigns supreme!

Jealousy Reminds Us That We're Not Doing It

If I'm thriving, my jealousy is non-existent. I will have no need to project negativity on anyone else because I'm already doing what I want. But if I'm not "doing it," and I witness someone doing what I want to be doing, watch out! Projection/jealousy will haunt me until I take action.

What follows is a quick story (did you know I like stories?!) which shows how jealousy helped me clearly identify a personal 'A' activity, one that I was capable of doing, but hadn't yet taken action.

Several years ago I went to a local Mexican restaurant with my friend, Barry, a fellow gringo. When the waitress came to our table, Barry started to joke with her in his obviously fractured Spanish. Rather than being amused by their humorous interchange, I was seething with anger. How could he be so arrogant? Why was he being so rude and leaving me out of the conversation? After the waitress left, he asked me several times what was wrong. But I didn't have a clue.

It wasn't until I got home and kept thinking about it that I recognized the real problem. It wasn't about Barry at all. I was jealous of what he was doing (and I was not), and realized that I wanted to be doing the same thing. And, it was realistic — if Barry could do it, so could I! The next day I signed up with a tutor to learn Spanish myself!

If we can learn how to appreciate and understand the power of projection, we will have another tool for discovering our 'A's. And jealousy, that often misunderstood emotion, can serve as a guiding light for what we truly want to be doing with our life.

A ddendum

Jealousy — Why It's Really About You

(*Psychology Today*, August, 2009)

Jealousy is beginning to be discussed as a "signal to look within." With introspection, the jealousy unleashed in a destructive path can instead be viewed as a valuable signal to look within and repair one's own sense of self. Jealousy often says more about the bearer than about the deeds or misdeeds of a mate.

French psychiatrist Marcianne Blevis, author of *Jealousy: True Stories of Love's Favorite Decoy*, sees jealousy "as a resource when we feel at risk, when our sense of self is put in jeopardy." Jealousy of a rival, then, often masks our craving for a part of ourselves that has been ignored. [In our story, jealousy is seen as a valuable resource for discovering the 'A' within **ourself** that is missing or has been ignored.]

Amusing Applications of Projection

Sometimes projection can work in a rather amusing and benign way. A while ago I conducted a simple experiment to see if people asking a question were, in fact, wanting to make a statement. If this were true, it would mean that they were really projecting on another what they were thinking/feeling, but camouflaged in the form of a question. Here's what I discovered:

Example #1: A colleague came bouncing up to me and asked, "Hey, what are you going to be doing this summer?" It appeared to be a simple straightforward question (!), but on the hunch that it had more to do with him than me, I merely asked him about his summer plans. His excited response, "Well, I just got a fellowship to study in London, and I'll be leaving in two weeks..." Guess who was never asked again about his summer plans?!

Example #2: A friend approached me and seemingly out of the blue (nothing is ever out of the blue) inquired about the status of my pride and joy, a restored '54 GMC Pickup. I was eager to respond, but thought that his question might really be a statement of what he wanted to talk about. Instead of answering, I asked, "So, what are you doing for wheels these days?" His quick response: "Well, I just test-drove the new Mini Cooper last night, and what a sweet ride..." And I didn't even get a chance to talk about my nifty '54!

Some space to doodle.

Listen to Your Body / Listen to Your Soul

" A sound mind in a sound body is a short but full description of a happy state in this world.

John Locke

One of the hallmarks of living a THRIVING 'A' life is to feel so passionate about your life's work that you would do it even if you didn't get paid for it. Well, almost anyway! Learning how to listen to your body and soul is a powerful way to discover your "it," your mission in life.

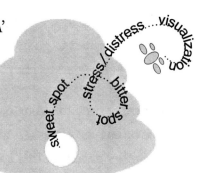

Listening to your body and soul is also a "twofer," able to give you both bitter and sweet advice about your best life path. That is, the listening can produce two opposite and important messages. It can tell you when something is in *flow* and therefore sweet (to be embraced), or when something is stressful and therefore bitter (to be repulsed). In brief,

Flow = The Sweet Spot $\therefore$ To Be Embraced

Stress/Distress = The Bitter Spot $\therefore$ To Be Repulsed

REFRESHER: In the Primer on 'A's and 'B's, we discussed Mihaly Csikszentmihalyi's concept of *flow* as the psychological state when you and your actions are "one." Flow occurs when you are stretching yourself toward meaningful challenges. This is the essence of performing 'A' activities and consequentially becoming a *THRIVING* 'A'.

A recent poignant interview with famous movie directors Ivan Reitman (*Ghost Busters*) and his son Jason (*Thank You for Not Smoking* and *Juno*) illustrates how listening to your body and soul can help in discovering your 'A's. As a young man, Jason had passionately followed his father around the movie sets. From this early age it was clear that in his heart Jason really wanted to go into the movie business. But he did not want to be type cast as a "daddy's boy" by following in his footsteps.

When it came time to make his career choice, he contemplated becoming a doctor or lawyer. He asked his father what he thought of these choices, and his father gave him this advice, "Son, there's no magic in it for you." Many of us are glad he chose to be a movie director!

> *"You must be nothing but an ear that hears what the universe of the world is saying constantly within you."*
> Rabbi Dov Baer of Mezritch

In this chapter, listening to the sweet spot (*flow*) will be described from three different perspectives--sports, art/music, and your inner soul. Each perspective will give a different view on how and what to embrace in your life. Next, I will discuss how listening to the bitter spot (stress/distress) can help you make important decisions, namely by helping you discover what you need to repulse and reject.

L isten to the Sweet Spot

The Sweet Spot in Sports

> *"The biomechanical genius of the body...those wonderful peak moments of movement when we are 'poetry in motion.'"*
> Dr. George Sheehan, author of *Running and Being*

I was introduced to the "sweet spot" concept in a sports psychology book by John Jerome, *The Sweet Spot in Time*. Jerome describes this spot as being when mind and body are synchronized in perfect athletic performance. When the physiological and psychological forces are at work to produce a moment of sheer sports perfection, that is the sweet spot.

If you've played any "stick-and-ball game", you're familiar with the wonderful sensation of hitting the sweet spot. When you hit it, there is a characteristic sound — a sharp click (golf), crack (baseball), or whack (tennis). And even more exciting is the inner feeling we experience.

Biomechanist Peter Cavanagh demonstrates in his lab that the sweet spot is not a figment of the imagination, but a biomechanical reality. We have specific self-sensing organs in our body called *propriocepters*. These internal measuring devices tell an athlete when he is hitting the internal sweet spot — the timing is right and the motion is smooth, the skill levels are higher, the athletic motions quicker, more forceful, and more accurate.

Jerome also stresses the importance of "taking the time." The good athletic performer takes all the time there is for a particular move. When in the sweet spot, time slows down, everything appears to be in slow motion, more vivid and more clear. Some go so far as to call it a "momentary healing of the mind-body split."

Although Descartes would like this characterization, it is probably a bit overstated! But what cannot be overstated is the true magic an athlete feels during a particularly fulfilling moment when "mind and body" seem to come together...this is what it means to experience the sweet spot in sports.

The Sweet Spot in Art/Music

"Finding the sweet spot is the process of discovering effortless mastery."
Kenny Werner

Finding the sweet spot in art/music is described by Kenny Werner as a process of "effortless mastery." In his book of the same title, he says the following,

"Mastery is playing whatever you're capable of playing...every time... WITHOUT THINKING..."

At performance time, the music plays itself while the musician observes. This is when music becomes easy--that's the secret.

In his Zen-like manner, Kerner talks about "letting go of fear," for fear prohibits you from revealing the music in your soul. With relaxed focus, practice and patience, the true music within you will appear. He says that mastery is comprised basically of two things:

1. Staying out of the way and letting music play itself; and

2. Being able to play the material perfectly every time without thought.

Although experiencing effortless mastery can sound a bit "new age" (you think?!), "finding your voice" is another way of saying that you've discovered your special 'A' purpose in life. Effortless mastery is that feeling you have when you are in tune with your unique strength and passion. Listen to that voice!

The Sweet Spot in Your Inner Soul

> *"Each person is given something to do that shows who God is."*
> I Corinthians 12.7 (MSG)

Prolific Christian author Max Lucado, in *Cure for the Common Life — Living in Your Sweet Spot*, is very clear in his main point — find your sweet spot; you have one!

He believes that God gives each of us a sweet spot — a zone, a region, a life precinct in which we were made to dwell. And you find it in your uniqueness. Examine and embrace your skills and you will discover your talents and abilities. Heed your "inner music" and you will find your "flow."

Lucado promotes a God-centered way to discover our sweet spot. He states simply that God endows us with gifts so we can make Him known.

The author implores us to use our uniqueness to make a big deal about God. This can often be found in the work we do. And whatever that work is, it matters to the world. We need plumbers, soldiers, repairmen and doctors. Whether we "log on" or "lace up" for the work day, we imitate God. Remember, says Lucado, God himself worked for the first six days of creation!

Since our career typically consumes half of our lifetime, God honors this work and expects us to honor Him in that work. Lucado sums up how to find your sweet spot in the following way:

Use your uniqueness (what you do)
to make a big deal out of God (why you do it)
every day of your life (where and when you do it).

By the convergence of your strengths, giving glory to God and living it every day, you will discover your sweet spot, your zone in which to thrive.

L isten to the Bitter Spot

In the beginning of this chapter I stated how listening to our body and listening to our soul is "bittersweet", a "two-fer." We have used ideas from sports, art/music and your inner soul to show how listening to the sweet spot can help us discover our 'A's.

Now we get to the other side of the coin — listening to the bitter spot. The cornerstone of the bitter is stress/distress. When our body and soul are out of alignment, it is a message that we are doing something that is **not** an 'A' activity. Recognizing the bitter is critical in learning what to repulse and rebuff in our life.

A Brief Primer on Stress and Distress

"Stress is an ignorant state. It believes that everything is an emergency."
Natalie Goldberg

Most succinctly, the best definition of stress is to be "keyed-up." Too little stress (not keyed-up enough) leads to boredom and too much stress (too keyed-up) typically leads to high anxiety, high blood pressure and the like.

Each of us may have widely differing experiences with stress, yet one thing is sure — what is going on with our mind and emotions is just as important as what is happening in our body. In fact, what is going on in our mind determines what is happening in our body.

The key point to remember about stress is the powerful influence it has on our mind and body. *Psychoneuroimmunology* is an exciting new field of study which seeks to understand the complex communications between the nervous system, the psyche, and the immune system, and their implications for health. But you don't need to be a card-carrying *psychoneuroimmunologist* (can you tell I like this word?!) to know when you are out of alignment because of stress. Listening to the bitter spot in our body and soul is key to understanding and discovering how we are doing in pursuing our 'A's.

Recognizing the Bitter Spot -- A Personal Experience

As I found out from personal experience, listening to our physiology can truly help us distinguish between 'A' and 'B' activities. When we are stressed out (either from being too keyed-up or not keyed-up enough) our bodies will tell us, if we just listen.

For years I had professed to others the importance of visualization in making important decisions. I finally decided to try it myself:

It was a balmy day as I prepared to relax the weekend away before beginning work at my new job in the Health Center at USC. Laying by the pool of my apartment complex, I noticed extreme gastrointestinal discomfort. At first I thought it was God punishing me for contemplating a slothful weekend! But it had to be more than that. I needed to know. Enter visualization.

I decided to use visualization to help me discover the source of my distress. Was I nervous about the training sessions for the new interns? What about teaching a new class in Counseling Education with limited time to prepare? Or, could it be my vacillation on whether or not to accept a lecture opportunity at the Dental School?

When I visualized the first two possibilities, nothing much happened. However, when I visualized the third possible choice, something *very* different happened. My internal organs felt like they were going to explode. I had found my bitter spot!

What I learned (again) about myself was my high need to please. There were many people who told me how honored I should feel for being considered to lead the lecture series. It may have been their 'A' activity, but it surely was not mine.

I turned down the lecture opportunity at the Dental School. Really listening to the "bitter" was the only way of discovering what to reject, and to understand that I was almost doing a *should* rather than a *want*.

The title of a well-known mind/body book says it all, "*YOUR BODY DOESN'T LIE.*" Finding the sweet spot (*flow*) in your body and soul is key to discovering your 'A's. Equally important, listening to the bitter spot (stress/distress) can help you decipher what is not an 'A' for you. In other words, if you really listen to your body/soul, you will be richly rewarded by gaining clarity in your decision-making process.

Oops. Another blank page.

Take Time to Muse

> You cannot see yourself in running water, only in still water.

> *Zen Proverb*

Muse has become one of my new favorite words! Maybe it's just the sound — *muse*. Reminds me of my love affair with the word *calm* — with both muse and calm I can imagine someone coming from another planet and instantly knowing what these words mean, just by their sound.

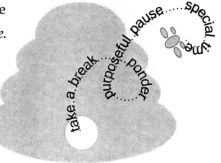

In its simplest form, to muse means to *ponder*. But its true meaning is so much richer and deeper. Musing is about stepping away from the frantic noise and clatter of life; moving from the "urgent" to those things that are truly "important" and matter the most. One author likens this process to leaving the crowded dance floor and retreating to the balcony in order to get a better view of what is really going on below.

Plotting our strategy to get away from the urgencies of life takes careful and purposeful planning. And the KILLER 'B's will not make it easy! Richard J. Foster, author of *Celebration of Discipline*, states it well:

"In contemporary society our Adversary majors in three things: noise, hurry, and crowds. If he can keep us engaged in 'muchness' and 'manyness,' he will rest satisfied."

The Many Faces of Musing

There are countless ways to find "still water" where you can clearly "see yourself" and discover clarity amidst the chaos. Here are a few powerful ways:

The Purposeful Pause

"Now come along to some quiet place by yourselves, and rest for a little while."
Mark 6.31 (New Testament)

Jesus understood the frenzy of life. People back-to backed his calendar with demands. But he also knew how to "step away from the game" and go to a deserted place to stay focused on his true purpose. This is how he handled an unruly crowd who wanted more and more of him as described in the Gospel of Luke from the *New Testament*.

Then, as the sun was setting, all those who had friends suffering from every kind of disease brought them to Jesus and he laid his hands on each one of them separately and healed them. Evil spirits came out of many of these people, shouting, "You are the Son of God."

But he spoke sharply to them and would not allow them to say any more, for they knew perfectly well that he was Christ.

At daybreak he went off to a deserted place, but the crowds tried to find him and, when they did discover him, tried to prevent him from leaving them. But he told them, "I must tell the good news of the kingdom of God to other towns as well — that is my mission."

And he continued proclaiming his message in the synagogues of Judaea.

Luke 4.40-44 (The New Testament in Modern English)

On numerous occasions Jesus removed himself from the clamoring crowds to re-focus, re-energize and re-chart his course of action. This often occurred while he was ministering to others but felt pulled in many different directions. He said *no* to many good things so he could say *yes* to his best thing — his unique mission.

Sister Theresa was also noted for her ability to take a purposeful pause each day. Ministering to the hoards of miserably poor people in Calcutta was a seemingly endless task. But each day, she instructed her assistants to guard against interruptions while she engaged in solitary prayer for two to three hours in the morning and evening. This is how she stayed focused on her unique call.

Yoga Meditation

"Meditate on whatever causes a revolution in your mind."
A Yoga Monk

Meditation is the act of listening. It requires that we descend into silence so we can *listen* to our inner voice of meaning and purpose. Most humanoids are burdened with what the Buddhists call the "monkey mind" — the thoughts that swing from limb to limb stopping only to scratch themselves, spit and howl! It probably doesn't sound very flattering to be reduced to "monkey minds," but when we take a closer look at how our minds constantly jump from thought to thought, we realize that we often don't give ourselves the opportunity to find a quiet place to truly discover who we are and what we want to be.

The goal of meditation is to teach us how to stay in the present moment. Different meditation techniques teach us how to stay focused — for instance, by focusing your eyes on a single point of light, or by observing the rise and fall of your breath. Most Yoga teachers use a mantra (sacred words or syllables) that is repeated in a focused manner.

And what is the main purpose of these mantras in meditation? Namely, to transport us to another state, rowboat-like, through the choppy waves of the mind. Whenever your thoughts get pulled into chaotic cross-currents, you can climb back into your rowboat and keep going. By keeping us centered and focused, meditation has exceptional power to help us discover our 'A's.

Much has been written about the process and power of meditation. Many of the above ideas on meditation were taken from Elizabeth Gilbert's delightful book, *Eat, Pray, Love*. If you are looking for an insightful and readable book on how to use yoga meditation as a way of discovering your 'A's, this could be a excellent place to start. There is good reason why it was a long-time New York Times Bestseller!

Retreats

Bill Gates recommends that all organizations take two retreats each year to focus on their vision, mission and purpose. Bill Gates!! He sees retreats as the only way for an organization to take time away from the daily busyness of business to review, re-chart, and refine its reason for being.

If the call for organizations to use retreats to stay focused is true, it is equally true for individuals. And, in order to stay focused on your mission, you must be crystal clear on what that mission is.

One of the major influences in writing this book was reading Stephen Covey's *The Seven Habits of Highly Effective People*. It was particularly inspirational to learn that he regularly uses personal retreats to discover and clarify what is important in his life. As you can tell from his numerous publications, he is a purposeful and 'planful' individual. For his personal retreats, he will typically go to a beautiful and secluded location for a designated period of time (often a week or longer) and systematically review where he wants to be going in his life. For all of us, a personal retreat can be a powerful way to first discover our 'A's and then continue to renew and refresh those 'A's on a regular basis.

A Break in the Action

For 10 years I traveled around the country doing stress seminars — that was, until I got burned out! The single most important thing I learned was the power of chronic stress, a condition that is debilitating when it is constant and unrelenting. The best way to break this vicious cycle is to take a moment to relax. Simultaneously, this relaxing pause can provide a time to refocus on your mission.

Sir Winston Churchill and Dr. Albert Sweitzer are two historical figures whose actions exemplify the benefits of taking breaks during stressful times. We'll start with the example of "Sir Winston."

During the height of World War II, Great Britain was in dire straights. The country was in grave danger of being destroyed or at least greatly damaged by the Nazi war machine. The British people were scared and nervous as they turned to their leader for support and guidance. Sir Winston felt the weight of responsibility and knew that he would have to make critical decisions to calm his people and chart the necessary direction to prevent his country's demise.

How did he discover the course of action to take? During the most critical times he regularly took a break from the action. Each afternoon he had his assistants draw a hot bath, bring him a glass of brandy and his ever-present cigar. In this tub he pondered the choices before him. Taking time to muse was crucial to his clear and decisive decision making.

Dr. Albert Sweitzer, famous for his medical intervention in Africa, also used a break in the action to stay focused on his mission and purpose. Seemingly endless lines of people waited for critical medical attention outside his make-shift medical tent. But several times a day he instructed his assistants to withhold entry of potential patients. Dr. Sweitzer would then retreat to a piano in the room and proceed to play for an hour or so. The one-time concert pianist used this break to stay refreshed and focused on his primary mission.

What Makes for Good Musing?

"If it's not in your day, it's not in your life."
Richard McCrary

Whether you are looking to discover, re-discover or re-chart your 'A's, the process of musing has several necessary qualities which must be practiced on a consistent basis. Basically, they include:

A Special Place

You will notice that each of the stars of musing cited above had a special place in which to ponder and refocus. The specific place is obviously very personal, but what is critical is to have that special place. Like Jesus, it could be a retreat to the desert for prayer. For practitioners of yoga meditation, it is usually guidance from a guru in a peaceful location. Stephen Covey uses the quiet and solitude of the Utah mountains. And Winston Churchill used the simple bath while Dr. Sweitzer took a break to play the piano.

A Special Time

If you simply think of musing as a good idea that can happen by wishful thinking or osmosis, you're wrong! To gain the potential power from musing you must definitely set aside specific time to muse. Although the special time you choose is personal and idiosyncratic, taking the time is not.

A Special Process

Wise people have long noted that there are "many roads to Mecca." Similarly, there are also many special processes to use for musing. I have illustrated just a few — prayer, meditation, retreats, or simply taking a break in the action.

What each of these processes have in common is ritual — a procedure that is regularly followed. The best advice is not to worry about finding the special place, time or process in which to muse, but to take the time to sample from a variety of options until you find what works for you.

My Acequia Muse

I live in Corrales, New Mexico — the Land of Enchantment! One of my special places to muse is along the historic and bucolic acequia (irrigation ditch) outside our home. Each morning I hitch up our Husky-mix puppy and head out the back gate to walk along the acequia. It was on one such walk that it "suddenly" occurred to me that my mission in life was to help people "learn to thrive," rather than merely survive. As a WORKER 'B' most of my life, I did not want to go to the grave "with the song still in me." I also assumed there were many of my fellow 'B's in the same boat who could benefit from ideas on how to thrive.

But for a long time what puzzled me the most was why the thrill of thriving alluded so many. When the notion that **WORKER 'B's are Susceptible to KILLER 'B's** popped into my head on one of these acequia muses, I knew that I wanted to share this idea with others.

Now that you know all about KILLER 'B's and WORKER 'B's (from the Primer on 'A's and 'B's) and you have the tools on how to discover your 'A's (Discovering Your 'A's), you are ready for the real work — Implementing Your

'A's. We will begin with the importance of your belief system and continue on with a number of principles that hopefully will make your 'A' journey enjoyable and productive.

Section Four
Implementing Your 'A's

Believe that You Can Change

> Whether you think you can or think you can't, you're right.
>
> *Henry Ford*

This chapter is all about mind-set, whether you believe in a *fixed mind-set* or a *growth mind-set*. If you are truly interested in implementing a master plan for THRIVING, it is imperative to believe that change is possible.

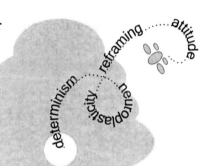

First, let's take a look at the fixed mind-set position.

Fixed Mind-Set

"In the adult centers the nerve paths are something fixed, ended and immutable."
Santiago Ramon y Cajal

A fixed mind-set means you believe intelligence and growth potential are bestowed at birth, and that no real change is possible after the age of five. If you see the world this way, you are not alone!

In fact, in the scientific community the textbook wisdom held that that the adult brain was hardwired, fixed in form and function, so that by the time you reach adulthood, you are pretty much stuck with what you have. This gloomy assessment is succinctly expressed by the Nobel Prize-winning Spanish neuroanatomist Santiago Ramon y Cajal in the quote above.

This view, called *neurogenetic determinism*, argues that there is a direct causal relationship between our genes and our behavior. Fueled by the mystique of modern genetics, new genes were constantly discovered "for" this and that behavior or mental illness. For example, if a woman is depressed it is because she has genes for depression; there is violence in the streets because people have violent or criminal genes; or, people get drunk because they have genes for alcoholism. This deterministic view is humorously expressed by one of comedian Flip Wilson's most outrageous characters, Geraldine, who says, "The devil made me buy this dress!"

Genetic predisposition should not be totally rejected as a determining factor in whether or not we can grow and change, but it is not the whole story. Enter the *growth mind-set* concept.

Growth Mind-Set

"If you can dream it, you can do it."
Walt Disney

Fortunately for those of us who want to Thrive and act upon our dreams, the dogma of neurogenetic determinism has been shown to be fundamentally wrong. It has been replaced by the *growth mind-set*, which says that "smarts" and change can be learned. Encouragement for this new way of thinking comes from an unusual ally — neuroscience. This branch of science is furnishing hard evidence that the brain is plastic, endowed with a lifelong capacity to reorganize itself by engaging in new experiences.

Numerous scientific discoveries have found that the brain can be rewired — it is neither static, nor fixed, but able to continually change. Not only can the brain learn new tricks, but it can also change its structure and function — even in old age. In fact, the adult brain can retain much of the plasticity that is characteristic of the developing child brain.

This study of the changing brain — *neuroplasticity* — has resulted in many stunning discoveries. More on that in a moment. Most relevant for our discussion on how to "implement our 'A's" is the fact that our hope for change is valid-- if our brains can change, we can change.

Baby Boomers will remember the cogent advice given to the Dustin Hoffman character in the classic 60's movie, *The Graduate* — the hope for your future is plastics! Now we can say that neuroplasticity is our hope for the future!! Change is possible; we can learn to thrive rather than merely survive.

E vidence for Neuroplasticity

"Who needs 'plastics' when you have 'neuroplasticity'!"
Alan Hedman

If you are looking for some of the most compelling and convincing evidence for the power of the brain to change, look no further than Sharon Begley's *Train Your Mind, Change Your Brain*. This treatise summarizes the 2004 summit meeting of the Dalai Lama and leading researchers on the topic of neuroplasticity. For example, neuroscientist Richard Davidson of the University of Wisconsin at Madison, presents evidence that many emotions previously believed to be fixed (like love and compassion) can dramatically be learned by intensive training. With his pioneering studies of brain scans on Buddhist monks, he has found physical evidence that brains can change and love and compassion can be learned.

In a more modest scientific experiment at Harvard Medical School, neuroscientist Alvaro Pascual-Leone had volunteers trooping into his lab to learn and practice a little five-finger piano exercise. After two hours of practice every day for five days, there was clear evidence of changes in the physical structure and function of the brain. When the experiment was repeated with the volunteers only visualizing the piano exercise (mental practice), similiar reorganization of brain patterns occurred.

Further evidence that mind-sets can be changed is presented by Carol Dweck, a Stanford University researcher in an experiment she ran on junior high math students. In the course of eight weeks she taught the students concepts like:

≈   Your brain is like a muscle that can be built up;

≈   You're like a baby who starts out knowing nothing and then learns; and,

≈   Everything is hard before it gets easy, so don't give up.

Then she tested the students to see if their grades improved. They did, by a lot. The students in the study group significantly outperformed their peers, many improving dramatically.

NOTE: If you are interested in another study on the evidence for neuroplasticity, see the addendum at the end of this chapter on improvisation.

The Gift of Reframing

"Attitude is everything; choose a good one!"
Swedish Proverb

Life is all about attitude. Our brain can help us change how we see the world. We can choose to give power to the situations we encounter in life OR we can choose how we want to view that situation. The following humorous story (fictional, I hope!) illustrates the power of attitude.

A family was very concerned about the psychological health of their two sons, one who seemed perpetually gloomy while the other seemed to be unduly positive all the time. To help figure out what was going on, they did what all good parents would do — engage the services of a psychologist to diagnose the situation. The psychologist performed the following experiment:

First, he brought the gloomy son into a large room filled with every imaginable toy. He instructed the boy to do whatever he wanted while the psychologist would be gone "for a while." Thirty minutes later upon his return, he found the boy morosely sitting in the corner. When asked why he wasn't playing with any of the toys, the boy replied, "If I started playing with any of them, some kid would probably just come along and take them away from me."

Soon thereafter the psychologist introduced the sunny boy to a gymnasium-sized room filled with three feet of horse manure. The psychologist said that he had to leave for a while and instructed the boy to do whatever he wanted. When the psychologist returned, he found the boy whistling and singing, gleefully throwing manure in the air. When asked why he was so happy, the boy simply responded, "With all this horse manure, there's got to be a pony in here somewhere!"

Whether we view a situation as positive or negative, scary or exciting, happy or sad, it's **all** based on how we *frame* it. And, if we initially see something as negative, we can reframe it into something positive; proof that "lemons can be turned into lemonade." I hope you are ready for another story, this time a true story on how reframing helped save a family trip.

An Adventure in Reframing - the Egyptian Story

Several years ago our family was treated to a once in a lifetime Christmas trip to Egypt. Our Egyptian hosts treated us to every kind of imaginable treasure. And because a horrible massacre of 180 Western tourists had occurred in November, 90% of the tourist trade had been cancelled. It was as though we had all the highlight areas to ourselves.

After a particularly blissful three days vacationing at the Red Sea with our friends, we had decided to visit Luxor on our own. But the only sensible way to go was via a four hour bus ride on local transportation. This meant being virtually the only non-Egyptians on a crowded bus with no restroom breaks, loud music, and chain-smoking passengers. I envisioned this as a disaster waiting to happen.

As I proceeded to be a nervous wreck, my wife remained cool and calm the entire ride. This came from someone who comes from a hyper-vigilant family, from someone who often reminds me that potential danger could be lurking around the next corner! When I asked her for the "secret" on how she remained so relaxed, she said it was simply a matter of seeing the bus ride as an *adventure*, something to be treasured rather than something by which to be traumatized by. Talk about reframing!

The Egyptian story and many similar situations have proved to be a good lesson for me in readdressing worry. As an Olympic caliber worrier, I had often been tortured by worries big and small. A caring friend once told me — "today's crisis is tomorrow's story!" This is not only true, but great advice to give one who loves stories as much as I do.

Change *is* possible but not easy. Therefore it is reassuring to know that we can change. The belief that we can change is clearly the *sine qua non* (ultimate prerequisite) for making change happen. Our mind can help us see positive where only negative exists. We can change our attitude. We can reframe. We can change from being a 'B' to becoming an 'A'.

With attention and mental effort, and a large dose of patience, we can indeed learn new habits and rituals to reach our goals. Patience is particularly difficult, which makes it very easy to get discouraged along the way. It is important to keep the big picture in mind and remember that all the hard work will ultimately pay off.

Gregg Popovich, coach of the NBA San Antonio Spurs, uses the following thought to encourage himself and his players to steadfastly continue on their journey.

> *"When nothing seems to help, I go look at a stonecutter hammering away at his rock, perhaps a hundred times without as much as a crack showing on it. Yet at the hundred and first blow it will split in two, and I know it was not that blow that did it, but all that had gone before.*
> (from Jacob Riis, 19th Century Reformer, "Stonecutter Credo")

I hope you're ready for some straight-forward suggestions on how to implement your 'A's. This is where we'll put together the partnership of thought, belief and action.

> *"If your mind can conceive it, your heart can believe it, then you can achieve it."*
> (from *Crisis Magazine*, Spring, 2008)

In the following chapters we will discuss the habits and rituals which can help you achieve your dreams. They include:

≈ Starting with your 'A's

≈ Surround yourself with other 'A's

≈ Find a "tough love" program

≈ Have fun even while being afraid

≈ Create a crisis

A ddendum

More Evidence for Neuroplasticity - Improvisation

"All That Jazz"

In an earlier chapter, we discussed how mastery enables a professional athlete, artist or musician to be in a state of mind called a *"zone"*, or what Csikszentmihalyi called *"flow"*. Another essential element of mastery and creativity is *improvisation*. Drs. Charles Limb and Allen Braun of the National Institute of Health wanted to find out what happens in the brain when a jazz pianist improvises.

In the study, the selected pianists played a simple scale as well as a more complex original jazz composition. The researchers were particularly interested in comparing how the brain functions during these two activities. They found a marked difference between the two conditions.

During improvisation, the medial prefrontal cortex (MPFC) became very active. This is the part of the brain most identified with helping a person develop "their sense of self." At the same time, the sides of the prefrontal cortex (PPC), which are more involved with conforming to rules rather than promoting free expression, remained less active.

This is all good news! It means that when you improvise you literally turn on the part of your brain that is most closely aligned with your aspirations (think *THRIVING* 'A' activities) while quieting neural centers that would otherwise hold you back (like *KILLER* 'B' behaviors). And there's more! During improvisation, structures in the brain associated with anxiety (the amygdala and the hippocampus) also remain relatively quiet.

The beauty of this study is the demonstration that we don't have to be slaves to anxiety and rule-based inhibitions. By trying something new and different (improvising), we can curtail the power of *KILLER* 'B's that prevent us from pursuing our cherished 'A' goals.

Start with Your 'A's

 The main thing is to keep the main thing the main thing.

Stephen Covey

If there were a First Commandment for implementing your 'A's, it clearly would be — **First Things First**. Peter Drucker, the wise and renowned management consultant, once observed that there are not 24 hours in a day but only two or three. The difference between an effective person and everyone else is the ability to use those few hours productively and "get the main things done."

These "main things" or the "things which matter most" are an apt description of 'A' list activities. On any given day or week, start with the 'A's rather than with the 'B's. It is often very comforting to successfully complete items from the 'B's To-Do list, but it will not help you reach the THRIVING 'A' level.

Around the time that Drucker was challenging us to get the main things done, E.M. Gray wrote an impressive essay entitled, *"The Common Denominator of Success"*. This was written after he had spent his work-life searching for the one common denominator shared by all successful people. And the result?

Gray found that one factor seemed to transcend all others — the ability to put "first things first." It wasn't hard work, good luck, or astute human relations (though these are all important) but the ability to *organize and execute around priorities.*

Perhaps the most recognized proponent of Starting with Your 'A's or putting first things first is, of course, Stephen Covey. In both The *Seven Habits of Highly Effective People* and *First Things First* he expounds on the familiar Pareto Principle — 80% of the results flow out of 20% of the activities. That is why he implores us to learn about the distinction between important priorities (THRIVING 'A' activities) and the host of compelling and sometimes apparently urgent matters (KILLER 'B' behaviors). Because of Covey's incredible importance in helping us understand how to implement our 'A's, the earlier reference to his work in the section on Primer on 'A's and 'B's is well worth reviewing.

The Passion of Vision and the Power of Goals

"A VISION without ACTION is a DAYDREAM;
ACTION without a VISION is a NIGHTMARE."
Alan Hedman

The Passion of Vision

"It is better to dare mighty things, to win glorious triumphs, even though checkered by failure, then to take with those poor souls who neither enjoy much nor suffer much, because they know not victory nor defeat."
Theodore Roosevelt

Teddy Roosevelt eloquently describes the passion of vision as the willingness "to dare mighty things." It is this kind of passion that becomes the starting point for implementing our 'A's.

Someone else who knew about the importance of vision was Viktor Frankel, an Austrian psychologist who survived the death camps of Nazi Germany. As both a participant and an observer of the Holocaust experiment, he was intrigued by the question of what made it possible for some people to survive when most died.

He analyzed several factors, including health, vitality, family structure, intelligence and survival skills. Finally, he concluded that none of these factors was primarily responsible. Rather, the most significant factor was the sense of a future vision. While an optimistic view of the future must be tempered with a hard, realistic evaluation of your present circumstances, the passion of vision is critical in keeping your "main thing" in clear focus.

"In the long run we only hit what we aim at."
Henry David Thoreau

The Power of Goals

"The most important thing about goals is having one."
Geoffry F. Albert

One writer has suggested that "if you don't know where you're going, any road will get you there." In other words, to get "there" you will need a plan. I know that for some people P-L-A-N is a "four-letter word," but in this case it's one of the good four-letter words. And, in order to effectively implement your *THRIVING* 'A' Plan you will also need SMART goals. The S-M-A-R-T goal paradigm is still one of the best (and simplest) ways to remember and implement your 'A' Plan. Here's a brief review of the idea:

S - Specific: Provide enough detail so that there is no indecision as to what exactly you should be doing when the time comes to do it.

Example of a poor goal: "Study biology"
Example of a better goal: "Read pp. 12-35 in biology text, write questions in the margins of the text, and practice answering those questions after reading."

M - Measurable: Your goal should be such that when you finish you have tangible evidence of successful completion.

Poor goal: "Read Chapter Three"
Good goal: "Read Chapter Three and then write a summary from memory."

A - Acceptable:	Your goal should be set by you rather than by someone else. AND, it should be directly related to your priority goals.
R - Realistic:	Plan to do things that are doable and that you are willing to follow through on.
T - Time Frame:	Say when you plan to work at your goal and when you will complete your goal.

When your SMART goals are wedded to the passion of your vision, you are headed in the right direction to implement your 'A's.

 Visual

The Pickle Jar Theory

Many of you are visual learners. Well, here's a visual, courtesy of Jeremy Wright, that can vividly help you picture (and remember) to start with your 'A's.

The Theory

Visualize an empty pickle jar. A wide-mouthed pickle jar in which you could fit at least three of the largest pickles you can imagine inside of it. Now, put in some large rocks until you think the jar is full.

Although you're quite sure your pickle jar is full, put some pebbles in. Put as many in as you possibly can. Then, take your "full" jar and put in some sand, until you can't possibly fit anymore in. Finally, add water.

The significance of this exercise and the symbolism herein is not terribly difficult to decipher:

≈ large rocks--our major goals and priorities

≈ pebbles--activities we enjoy doing

≈ sand--other activities we have to do

≈ water--those activities that simply clutter up our lives and seem to get in everywhere

Each of these items have their place. After all, we need the gamut of life experiences from major priorities to times of rest to feel truly balanced. According to the Pickle Jar Theory, the beauty of life is in this balance. We will be able to make time for all things important IF will follow the proper order.

The Anti-Theory

Of course there may be detractors of this visualized experiment, particularly those who have never actively practiced starting with their 'A's on a daily basis. And, who feel they are productive and get "enough" done.

But try this. With an empty pickle jar again, fill it with water until it is completely full. Now try and add some sand, pebbles and/or large rocks and observe what happens.

HINT: I've tried this for real and there's just not enough room for any large rocks. In symbolic terms, when you start with *KILLER* 'B's (water, sand or pebbles), there will be no room for your *THRIVING* 'A' activities (large rocks).

Essence of the Pickle Jar Theory

This theory is not designed to be subtle. But if you can ensure that your large priorities are tackled first, the results will be profound. And, there will still be time for the less profound things that add fun and spice to your life.

 Real-Life Example

Starting with your 'A's - Rabbi Laura Geller

While working at the Health and Counseling Service at USC (for those of you in the South, that's the University of Southern California!) I met a remarkable young rabbi named Laura Geller, the rabbi at Hillel House. Over the course of several years we had a number of enjoyable lunch meetings together. On one occasion she informed me that she needed to curtail these meetings for three - six months because she planned on an intense study of the Torah.

At first I felt hurt; I had been relegated to a 'B' Level activity! But then I saw the power of what she was doing. By starting with a clearly defined 'A' activity, she was able to accomplish profound results that would have been impossible without letting go of some 'B' activities.

At that time in my life I was a "high-end Survivor" (or maybe a low-end THRIVER!). Laura's example was an important lesson and had a profound effect — in order to truly Thrive I would have to start with my 'A's.

Maintaining Your 'A's

"A woodpecker can tap 20 times on 1000 trees and get nowhere, but stay busy. Or, he can tap 20,000 times on one tree and get dinner."
from The Dip (Daniel Pink's website)

Disciplined Thought and Disciplined Action

"If I chase two rabbits, each will escape."

Anyone can become an 'A' for the day! Well, almost anyone. But becoming a THRIVING 'A' cannot be reached by attainment alone; 'maintainment' is the true key to success. Maintenance is about having a relentless and persistent focus on a clearly defined vision and goal.

Given the power of urgency and crisis (plus the other assorted KILLER 'B's), maintenance is tough. My favorite examples to illustrate the degree of difficulty in maintenance are diet and exercise. How many people with perfectly good intentions join a diet program or exercise club, only to drop out soon thereafter (how's that for a rhetorical question?!)? Gyms, in fact, rely on a 60-70% no-show rate to prevent over-crowding and still survive financially.

To maintain the disciplined thought and disciplined action necessary to achieve 'A'ness, I would like to suggest two images and several "rules" to follow.

Images to keep in mind

Jim Collins (*Good to Great*) provides us with wonderful images for disciplined thought and action. He borrows inspiration from Isaiah Berlin's famous essay on *The Hedgehod and the Fox* to depict the piercing clarity of thought necessary to maintain 'A' activity. Remember, the fox is noted for being multi-talented and scattered, whereas **hedgehogs** have a simple, coherent concept of what they want to be and do. This *"Hedgehog Concept"* is an excellent image to keep in mind for maintaining disciplined thought.

This reminds me of the famous folktale involving the race between the tortoise and the hare. The hare, although speedy, gets distracted and is not consistent in his efforts. It is the tortoise, slow and steady and focused on one goal, who wins the race!

Collins uses the image of a **flywheel** to illustrate the concept of disciplined action. In becoming an 'A,' there is no single defining action, innovation, lucky break or miracle moment to credit. Rather, it's the constant, relentless action, not unlike turning a giant, heavy flywheel. With great effort, the slow and almost imperceptible progress will surely occur... Therefore, cherish the image of the lowly hedgehog when you need help on maintaining disciplined thought. And don't forget the image of the ponderous and unwieldy flywheel when you need help with disciplined action.

"Rules" to Follow

This is the math portion of our story on maintaining your 'A's! Malcolm Gladwell, of *Blink* and *The Tipping Point* fame, introduces us to the 10,000 Hour Rule in his latest book, *Outliers*. He examines the keys to success, stating that researchers have settled on what they believe is the magic number for true expertise or even greatness: *ten thousand hours*. At first this may seem like a daunting and insurmountable task, but do the math. If you apply roughly 10-20 hours per week to 'A' activities, you will be an unstoppable 'A' person in 10-20 years. How else would you like to spend your time?!

Remember Steven Sample's *70/30 Formula* for leadership from an earlier chapter? This formula suggests that up to 30% of a leader's time can be spent on substantive, 'A' activities. For you non-math majors, this leaves 70% of your time for dealing with the routine and urgent matters of life.

Stephen Covey, discussing the same idea, indicates that 20% of our time spent on important matters will result in maintaining 'A' behavior and action. Whether you choose 20% or 30%, these percentages seem to be in the same ballpark.

The Hedman Rule

Personally, I subscribe to the Hedman Rule (!): Anyone hankering to be a *THRIVING* 'A' person will need to commit to a critical mass of 10+ hours of 'A' activities *per week*. From very personal experience, I learned that if I didn't spend a minimum of 10 hours every week on this book, I became discouraged and distracted. And, the pain of repeatingly "starting the flywheel" was almost insurmountable. It was the 10+ hours that seemed to be the magic number for keeping me excited and motivated.

NOTE: If 10+ hours per week is the magic number, 40+ hours is not four times more magical! Other activities that are simply for fun and entertainment are necessary for balance in your life. A 40+ hour per week diet exclusively of 'A' activities is a recipe for discouragement, loneliness and burnout.

The following two chapters are also primarily about maintaining your 'A's. We continue with a discussion on the importance of "surrounding yourself with other 'A's" and "finding a 'tough love' program."

Yep - another blank page!

Surround Yourself with Other 'A's

Tell me who you're running with and I'll tell you who you are.

Quixote

No one will ever be able to live a THRIVING 'A' life without help from others. This involves learning about what to avoid and what to embrace. Whether we are talking about what to read and watch or who we should hang with, one question is imperative:

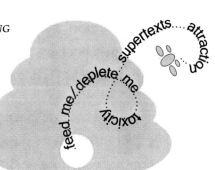

Does it feed me OR does it deplete me?

What to Avoid

Whatever or whoever depletes me.

Avoid Toxicity

"Even a little dab of toxicity is bad for you!"
Alan Hedman

Let me ask you a rhetorical question: "If I offered you an apple with 'just a little bit' of arsenic in it, would you accept?" I don't think so, and for obvious and good reasons — toxicity can kill you, even a little bit.

But let me ask you a similar question about the people in your life: "Do you spend time with family or friends who deplete you or are toxic?" In this case the answer for many is often quite different — he's been my best friend since high school, so... or, she's my sister, after all, and... As if, in this case a 'little toxicity' is not all that bad.

Dr. Susan Forward in *Toxic Parents: Overcoming Their Hurtful Legacy and Reclaiming Your Life* pulls no punches — anything that kills your self-worth or cripples you emotionally must be avoided. In the same vein, anything toxic will deplete you and thereby curtail the successful journey to a THRIVING 'A' life.

Avoid "Pity Parties"

"It's hard to soar with eagles when you're flying with turkeys."

If you specialize in surrounding yourself with those who have a victim mentality, or who simply don't bring out the best in you, it will be impossible to Thrive. Unfortunately, many people are more comfortable with failure than success, misery over happiness, and survival vs. thriving. These "rescue experts" can be very helpful when you're drowning, but not so helpful when you want to learn how to swim.

Many people in my psychotherapy profession seem to be most comfortable with people when they are "drowning." They are genuinely supportive with issues of pain and sorrow, but not so much with growth and development. This was made clear to me one time when a new referral said to me: "I'm coming to you because I heard you had no interest in 'pity parties,' whereas my previous therapist was absolutely wonderful and supportive when I talked about my deep pain, but seemed to be uncomfortable when I requested to learn ways to be healthy and happy."

One of the most painful and poignant descriptions of being more comfortable with failure and pain is portrayed in the 1979 indie movie, *Breaking Away*. In this coming of age film about four young men obsessed with cycling and struggling to grow up, one member decides to seek admission to an 'A' school for college. When asked by one of his friends how his father felt about this admission opportunity, he replied, "Actually, my father hopes I fail so he can comfort me." OUCH!

Similar to comfort in times of despair or failure is the notion of being mesmerized by rescue missions. Old-time readers of this book will remember the highly popular TV show of the '50's, *Lassie*. In each episode someone in the family suffered a tragedy and Lassie would come running to the rescue. One of the most famous of these rescue missions was preceded by a family member pleading the now often parodied line, "Timmy has fallen in the well and can't get out."

I firmly believe that comforting those experiencing sorrow is a special gift and that rescuing in time of failure or danger is to be honored. But, being with people who are more comfortable in a culture of surviving and focusing solely on rescue missions will deplete you. AND, prevent you from implementing your 'A's.

Avoid Boring People

What can I say, I like the title of Nobel Prize-winning James Watson's book, *Avoid Boring People*. (**DISCLAIMER**: I have big problems with his widely publicized remarks about race and intelligence, and found his rambling details of the "lessons learned from a life in science" to be mostly mean-spirited and incomprehensible.)

BUT, I think he has a point about boredom. Being around people who bore you is a good sign that you are probably not with someone who brings out the best in you. Also, not boring others requires that you make sure that you are not boring yourself. Boredom, then, is like the "dead canary in the coal mine," warning you of imminent danger. If you find yourself bored with others and/or yourself, it is a clear sign that you are feeling depleted and need to embrace "being fed."

What to Embrace

Whatever and whoever feeds me.

> "No one — not rock stars, not professional athletes, not software billionaires, and not even geniuses — ever makes it alone."
> Malcolm Gladwell, author of *The Tipping Point*

Gladwell, in his latest book, *Outliers*, seeks to define how people become successful, and to debunk the great American myth of the gifted, self-made man as the answer. He tells the sad, strange story of Christopher Langan, a man who despite an IQ of 195 (Einstein's was 150) wound up working on a horse farm in rural Missouri. "Why isn't he a nuclear rocket surgeon," asks Gladwell? Because of how he grew up: there was no one in Langan's life and nothing in his environment that helped him capitalize on his exceptional gifts. Therefore, he had to make his way alone.

What is it then, that we need to do, what we need to 'embrace' in order to implement our 'A's and Thrive? These following three ways are examples of how we can "feed ourselves."

Embrace What You Read

"You are the same today that you are going to be in five years from now except for two things: the people with whom you associate and the books you read."

Charles "Tremendous" Jones

I know nothing about "Tremendous," but would like to meet him some day because he nails the notion of whom and what we need to embrace. We have already touched on the "whom," so here are some thoughts on the "what."

Earlier in this book you were introduced to the thoughts of Steven Sample (*The Contrarian's Guide to Leadership*). He is a strong advocate of carefully choosing what you read. In his chapter entitled, "You are What You Read," he poses the following challenge: "If given a choice between reading the *New York Times* and *The Prince*, by Machiavelli, common wisdom would say to read the *New York Times*. Contrarian wisdom: read *The*

Prince." This book, along with other "supertexts," contains timeless truths about human nature. These timeless truths are the food that will help nourish you on your THRIVING journey.

Sample engaged in an interesting personal experiment. For 30 days he limited himself to 10 minutes per day of reading light material (newspapers, magazines, and the like) and 20 minutes for books, especially the supertexts. His conclusion? A total of 20 minutes a day translates into 120 hours a year, which equals 12+ books. I checked the math, and it works!

HIS ADVICE: make a conscious choice about what you choose to read.

This also applies to what we choose to view on television, on the Internet, and at the movies. In other words, "Watch what you watch!" By making a conscious choice to read and watch the best, we are in essence surrounding ourselves with the 'A' material that will help us implement 'A' results.

Embrace "The Law of Attraction"

> "*Basically put, the law of attraction says that* **like** *attracts* **like**. *But we're really talking at a level of thought.*"
> Bob Doyle, author

The ongoing runaway best seller, *The Secret,* describes the "law of attraction" as the Great Secret of Life. Basically, the law of attraction says like attracts like, so when you think a thought, you are also attracting like thoughts to you. The law of attraction is giving you exactly what you are thinking about — period!

Keep in mind that thoughts are magnetic, and that thoughts have a frequency wave. This means that whatever thoughts you have will attract all like things that are on the same frequency. Therefore, when you feel bad, you are on the frequency of drawing more bad things. When you choose to feel good, you are powerfully attracting more good things to yourself.

It is vital that you see yourself as being a human transmission tower, transmitting a frequency with your thoughts. When you want to change something in your life, start by changing your thoughts, which will inspire positive actions.

The application to "Implementing Your 'A's" is obvious:

Focus on your 'A' activity

Choose to put good thoughts towards this activity

Good thoughts will attract 'A' action and behavior

Thriving 'A' life will follow

"Remember, your current thoughts are creating your future life."
from *The Secret*

Embrace Other 'A's

"It takes a village to educate/feed a child."

Although this is an over-used quote, it's true. It means we can't implement our 'A's alone. If we want to "soar with the eagles" we need to spend quality time with other 'A's. Individually, this means identifying 'A' people that we want to be part of our "village," our team. Invite them to share, challenge and support our dreams.

We can also embrace other 'A's in a group context. I used to believe that 'A' writers and artists, for example, worked exclusively in solitude. Isn't it true that no great literary work or painting was ever done by committee?! Yes, the actual writing and painting was normally done solo. But, the necessary support to fully implement the dream often came from an ongoing advisory team. Check out the powerful impact Impressionist artists had on each other as they met and shared their artistic endeavors. And what about the numerous formal and informal writers' groups that meet on a regular basis for the purpose of improving each writer's work?

For the past 10+ years I've had the privilege of facilitating a high-level group of Nonprofit CEO's in a monthly meeting. The goal is to help each member realize his or her personal and professional dreams. By having a personal "team of advisers," each member is better able to implement 'A' activities.

One professional I know well is following the principle of surrounding himself with 'A's, both by creating an 'A' environment and by actively seeking out other 'A's to challenge and support him. His story describes a great way to consciously develop and implement 'A' activities.

R ob's Story

Those *KILLER* 'B's are truly sneaky and insidious. No wonder it is easy to lose your way toward an 'A' life.

A while back, I found myself working really hard on several projects and feeling pretty good about my accomplishments. I was exceeding my clients' expectations — creating some good stuff. And did I mention, I was working really hard; surely that is a commendable thing. I was not able to — scratch that — I *chose not to* give any time to my 'A' project, a program that challenges good teachers to be outstanding. The result: my venture took a backseat to these other projects. It made sense to give my focus to my clients' work; after all, they were challenging and important. And best of all, they were paying gigs!

It took a work-free weekend with friends for me to realize that I was — once again — a victim of the *KILLER* 'B's. I am fortunate to have a set of really good friends, all of whom are leading 'A' lives. They embrace challenges, focus on growth, and achieve their stretch goals. The weekend was spent talking about our ideas, our goals. We took turns challenging each others' assumptions. We engaged in wildly creative conversations where fresh ideas constantly popped up. We even came up with innovative ways to continue these discussions.

By the end of the weekend, I was so jazzed that I could hardly stand it. I could see that my 'A' activities are the ones that excite me. The projects on which I was working were great, but they were for my clients, not for me. I likened it to the person who crafted the frame for "Mulberry Tree" by Vincent Van Gogh. While I am sure the frame is wonderful and really accents the painting, it is Van Gogh's work that I remember. I want to be the artist!

I learned that it was easy for me to find comfort in 'B' activities. But a small taste of being with 'A's was all it took to realize just how unappetizing a 'B' life is for me. I am constantly reminded that it takes effort, discipline, and a plan to surround yourself with 'A' folks - a key toward living an 'A' life.

For a concrete method on how to implement your 'A's on a regular basis, see **Feed My 'A' List** on the following page.

A ddendum

Rob's Feed My 'A' List

After my 'A' weekend, I realized that I needed to find a better way to focus on my 'A's on a regular basis. I began by writing down my 'A' goals every morning before doing anything else. This worked for a while, but I soon found that simply writing them down was not enough. I needed to post my planned 'A' activities and goals somewhere public. Even if no one ever looked at them, I would still feel more accountable and less likely to let them slip by.

My solution was to create a blog. Unlike true blogs, I don't have anything fancy. I just write my goals for the week - short and sweet. I began the Feed My 'A' List blog writing goals daily, but this quickly proved to be too much work, so I moved to weekly posts. This is right for me. Every Monday, I begin my week by describing what 'A' activities I want to accomplish in the next seven days.

Feed My 'A' List has not been a magic bullet. I still rely on a "tough love" program (see the next chapter) and manipulate my schedule to spend more time with 'A' folks and less with 'B's. But posting my goals to the blog does ensure that I have a weekly reminder of what is important.

Image of Fresh Snow...

Find a "Tough Love" Program

> Do the best you can with what you have and do it now!
>
> *Theodore Roosevelt*

Have you ever wondered why there are so many gyms and personal fitness trainers? Wouldn't it be easier, equally effective and a whole lot cheaper to just do it on your own? There are, in fact, good reasons for working with a coach or mentor rather than trying to do it without help.

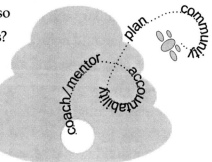

Sometimes we simply need a push to get started in the right direction as well as to maintain momentum. Also, we are social creatures and often don't work our hardest without a little "assistance" from a coach who loves us but will also continually push us toward excellence.

From the last chapter, "Surround Yourself with Other 'A's," I hope it is now crystal clear that in order to successfully implement your 'A's you need to constantly be with 'A' programs and 'A' people. The common denominator of all 'A' programs and people is **tough love**. But what are the attributes of successful tough love programs? And, why do so many people believe that we need a coach in order to attain and maintain our 'A' goals? Finally, is there truly a personal and professional payoff to coaching that makes the time and effort worthwhile?

The answers to these questions are next.

 ## Attributes of a Successful Tough Love Program

> *"The highest form of love is to have high expectations of another and hold them accountable."*
> Psychiatrist Alvin Pouissant

If you're not familiar with the concept of tough love, a brief description with examples should help. Early on, Alcoholics Anonymous (AA) realized that keeping recovering alcoholics on the right track often required getting tough while maintaining a spirit of love and acceptance. Below are two examples of tough love from the world of AA.

1. An individual has repeatedly borrowed money from a friend in order to satisfy his addictions. And, despite many sad stories and promises to repay as soon as possible, the individual continues to request money just "one more time." With *tough love*, the friend is to absolutely give no more money until the debt is repaid and the individual is clean and sober.

2. An adult child is again living at home after encountering many problems with drugs and alcohol that result in the loss of his job and apartment. But while living at home the child continues his addictive behavior and breaks house rules. According to the tenets of *tough love*, the parents are instructed to change the locks to the house, tell their child they love him dearly, and that he will be welcomed back only after he demonstrates sobriety and a willingness to follow family rules.

Tough love got its start in AA, but has rapidly spread to other arenas. For example, on the Oprah show, Dr. Pouissant (quoted above) and Bill Cosby discussed how tough love can be used with inner city kids failing in school and in life. They explained that having limited or low expectations was really a form of non-love, basically telling the student he was incapable of achieving very much of anything. Therefore, they suggested that the highest form of love was to have high expectations and support the student in reaching those expectations.

As you can see, there are two primary components of *tough love*:

A plan

Remember the "passion of vision" and the "power of goals" discussion in "Start with Your 'A's?" The main point that needs to be added here relates to the type of goals in a tough love program. Namely, the identified goals are usually stretch goals, those which require an individual to go outside his/her comfort zone. In order to determine if the goal is outside your comfort zone you can ask yourself these questions: does this goal make me and/or others a bit uncomfortable? does the thought of implementing the goal make me "wince"? (More details on "wincing" when I describe the *Decision-Making Model for Risk-Takers* in an upcoming chapter.)

Someone to hold us accountable

Even if you have a wonderful plan with great 'A' goals, you probably won't successfully implement your plan without a person and/or program to hold you accountable. It's not so much a question of will power but rather a fact of life that we all look to others for guidance. If humans were able to accomplish goals solely on their own, we wouldn't need schools or teachers!

Coaches can earn their money simply by being available on a regular basis to make sure their clients have done what they said they were going to do. This speaks to the importance of accountability. But hopefully, coaches do a lot more than merely "show up!" Good coaches support AND challenge us in our pursuit of 'A' goals.

Finding a Coach (Vizier, Mentor, Guru, or Community)

"Coaching: Lifting individuals beyond their comfort zone."
Training + Development (August, 2008)

Probably the biggest challenge is finding the right coach/mentor. The following discussion on the wide variety of coaching possibilities and the attributes that cut across all good coaching should help in this search.

A Brief History

Coaching has been around for a long time, with many different historical and cultural roots. I first became aware of coaching via the concept of a **vizier**. During medieval times, monarchs often needed sage advice when making important decisions (sounds rather current, doesn't it?). Should they turn to family members, who may have ulterior motives for their input? Not such a good idea! Rather, they often turned to an unbiased wise person who had no personal agenda and could give the monarch feedback he was not likely to receive from any other source. The vizier was a "truth-teller," a coach capable of telling the monarch what he needed to hear rather than solely what he wanted to hear.

From a different perspective, Rabbi Naomi Levy, in *To Begin Again*, describes the ancient rabbinic teaching that urges every person to have a **mentor**, or master. She likens it to "opening our eyes" to the sage advice by which we can learn from someone who is wiser than we are, someone who also has more experience, objectivity and insight. The mentor can share a peer perspective on life that we might never have arrived at on our own.

Many people have turned to eastern philosophies to find a "coach." *In Eat, Pray, Love,* Elizabeth Gilbert discusses her experience of going to India in order to study Yoga and to find union — between mind and body. The Yogic path is about disentangling the built-in glitches of the human condition. She understood some of the basic concepts, but how could she put that understanding into practice 24 hours a day? That's when she decided to employ the services of a **Guru**, a teacher for learning Yoga. She found out that in India it is considered standard operating procedure that you need a Guru. You come to a Guru with the hope that the merits of your teacher will reveal to you your own hidden greatness. Gandhi himself always wanted to study with a Guru, but never, to his regret, had the time or opportunity to find one. "I think there is a great deal of truth," he wrote, "in the doctrine that true knowledge is impossible without a Guru."

It is in the business sector of the Western world where coaching has been most closely discussed and analyzed. At one time coaching was used primarily for executives in trouble, and now it is mostly considered a perk for high quality performers. These executives are encouraged to engage the services of an executive coach in order to stay sharp and focused on their primary goals.

NOTE: If you are interested in a review of the literature on the ROI (Return on Investment) of coaching in the business world, check out the addendum at the end of this chapter, "Coaching: the Payoff."

The last variation of coaching that I will describe is **community**, or team coaching. This is when you have your own personal "team of advisers" who can coach you from the perspective of "walking in your moccasins." Whether it is a fellow team of writers, painters, or executives, the synergistic input of team members can be a very insightful and powerful process.

Attributes of a Good Coach

"Good coaches **challenge** *when courage is needed,* **support** *when encouragement is needed."*
Alan Hedman

So, do you like the idea of using a tough love coach? If you do, finding the best match is still extremely challenging. It really is a "match.com" world out there, with a seemingly endless stream of choices. Fortunately, there exists a certain commonality of attributes that distinguish good coaches.

Here is what a variety of experts on coaching have to say about these common attributes:

"The right mentor is someone who will lead us to insight and teach us wisdom, not someone who will predict our futures or tell us exactly what to do. A mentor seeks not to own us but to gently support us."
(from Naomi Levy, To Begin Again)

"A good Guru (coach) will reveal to you your own hidden greatness."
(from Elizabeth Gilbert, Eat, Pray, Love)

"People need a coach with credibility and one who can engender trust in the coaching relationship. Coaches should provide a high level of stretch that takes clients beyond their comfort zones."
(from "Coaching High Achievers," Consulting Psychology Journal, vol 48)

"Effective coaches are able to provide a confidential, caring and safe environment; be a generous and astute listener; act as a catalyst for change; be a "truth-teller;" provide focus and discipline in achieving goals; and also, help overcome resistance when roadblocks to achieving goals are encountered."
(from Alan Hedman's summary of How a Coach Helps an Executive.)

It should be clear that regardless of the "title," your coach/mentor is someone who challenges you to reach higher, and is there for you when you feel scared to move forward. The search process to find the coach who is best for you should be thorough, for having the right match will result in a rich and rewarding relationship.

Okay, so you've found an excellent tough love program and coach and feel confident that nothing can hold you back from successfully reaching your 'A' goals. Not so fast, campers! Never under-estimate the power of KILLER 'B's. You will probably be afraid when attacking your KILLER 'B's and contemplate retreating from your 'A' journey. Our next chapter is designed to help you actually have fun in this fearsome battle with the 'B's. Read on!!

A ddendum

Coaching: the Payoff

"A coach may be the guardian angel you need to rev up your career."
Money Magazine

Sometime ago in my work as an executive coach, I wondered what the professional literature had to say about the ROI for coaching. In a paper entitled, *Executive Coaching: The Payoff*, I reported my findings. Here is a brief summary of some research findings and "testimonials" that I found most persuasive.

Fortune Magazine, "Executive Coaching--With Returns a CFO Could Love," (February 19, 2001) conducted a survey with executives in which they asked for a conservative estimate of the monetary payoff from the coaching they received. The executives reported an average return of more than six times what the coaching had cost their companies.

"Coaching enhances the impact of executives, increases their speed in becoming effective within the organization, and improves overall job satisfaction. It is an especially useful tool at the executive level because busy

executives have few other assisted means of continued development."
(From The Case for Executive Coaching, *Business Magazine Chemistry*,
November, 2001)

Research from Case Western Reserve University's Weatherhead School of
Management shows that the impact of coaching can last seven years, as
compared to the benefits of seminar-heavy training which often vanishes
within a few months. (*Business Week*, November 11, 2002)

A study of Fortune 1000 companies found that executives using coaching
reported benefits to their leadership in the areas of increased productivity
(by 53%), increased retention of senior people (by 39%), reduction in costs
(by 23%) and increased bottom line profitability (by 22%).

The same survey reported improvements in their working relationships
with direct reports and their managers, team-building and business relationships with clients. (*Manchester Review*, 2001)

"The investment for executive coaching can pay off many times over--in-
creasing your bottom line, helping you work with renewed passion, working smarter, and reclaiming your life by adding more work-life balance."
(J.E. Auerbach, 2005 — *Seeing the Light: What Organizations Need to Know
About Executive Coaching*)

Finally, *Harvard Business Review* ("Manage Your Energy, Not Your Time,"
October, 2007) reported on how using executive coaches in an "energy
renewal program" boosted productivity at Wachovia Bank. Employees
participating in the program outperformed a control group of employees,
demonstrating significantly greater improvements in year-over-year performance during the first quarter of 2006.

NOTE: Future research will probably focus on **double bottom-line results**, which evaluates both professional and personal goals. With this methodolgy the payoff of coaching will not focus solely on the financial bottom line. Tough love programs will again have a valuable role to play.

Be Very Afraid AND Have Fun

> You don't want to descend into death slowly and resignedly. You want to continue racing through your exciting life, skid into the grave in a magnificent slide, yelling, 'What a ride!'
>
> *An Australian Saying*
> *(courtesy of Bert Witt)*

Making the fundamental changes necessary to live your dream can be foreboding. David L. Stein says it well, "The past is gone, the present is full of confusion, and the future scares the hell out of me!"

This section is all about the paradox of seemingly contrary and/or mutually exclusive ideas and principles that can help us implement our goals. For example, how can we simultaneously have fun while we're attacking a deadly killer? Or, how can we feel full-bodied fear and still take action? And, how can laughter and humor be powerful weapons in the fight with KILLER 'B's?

Don't be fooled; dealing with KILLER 'B's is not child's play. Sometimes the 'B's will be so subtle as to be almost imperceptible. At other times we may experience bone-rattling terror as we approach our new 'A' activities. Whether we are dealing with KILLER 'B's that are subtle slayers and must be flushed out into the open or KILLER 'B's that produce instant fear, the trick is to stay on course and take action.

The "Just Do It" slogan from Nike can serve as a good reminder. We can also take to heart poems like this from Guillaume Apollinaire:

We Can't.................................We're Afraid

Come to the edge.

We can't. We're afraid.

Come to the edge.

We can't. We will fall.

Come to the edge.

And they came.

And he pushed them.

And they flew.

One of the most under-used and/or under-appreciated tools in attacking KILLER 'B's and reaching our THRIVING 'A' goals is having fun while simultaneously being filled with fear. This is not a usual pairing, but a discussion on the importance of understanding the paradox should help. Then we will be ready to discuss two different ways of having fun while attacking KILLER 'B's, namely, *working hard at play* and *laughter yoga*.

The Power of Paradox

"Feel the fear and do it anyway."
Susan Jeffers

Susan Jeffers, in her fun and useful self-help book of the same name as the quote above, implores us to feel fear intensely AND take action anyway. Fundamentally, we must address one key question: can we *handle* the fear that automatically comes with taking risks? By imagining the "worst that could happen," we almost always realize that we can move forward. And, maybe even have fun along the way!

Other authors have identified powerful paradoxes that can inspire us to take action where we once found excuses or felt too afraid to move. Here's a sample of such writings:

"Once we know that life is difficult, then life is no longer difficult."
M. Scott Peck

Life, Difficulty and Truth

In M. Scott Peck's masterpiece, *The Road Less Traveled*, the author observes the following:

"Life is difficult. This is a great truth, one of the greatest truths. It is a great truth because once we truly see this truth, we transcend it. Once we know that life is difficult — then life is no longer difficult. Because once it is accepted, the fact that life is difficult no longer matters."

How zen-like, but true! For our purposes, it is important to remember that THRIVING is difficult, and that KILLER 'B's are fear-provoking. But battling the 'B's doesn't have to be all doom and gloom; it is also "legal" to have some fun and happiness as well.

Change and Happiness

Ten years ago, millions of readers were amused by Spencer Johnson's charming little allegory, *Who Moved My Cheese?!* But this book was written for more than charm and amusement. There is also a serious message: in order to change we must learn how to be happy. As the author states, "when you stop being afraid, you feel good."

In a seeming contradiction, BOTH fun and fear need to be embraced, BUT, fun needs to be in charge! As Johnson puts it, "There's only room for one in the driver's seat."

Brutal Facts and Optimism — The Stockdale Paradox

In a much more serious vein is the paradox introduced by Jim Collins in *Good to Great*. From an interview with General James Stockdale, a survivor of harsh punishment as a Vietnam P.O.W., Collins came to a powerful truth. Stockdale survived by retaining an unwavering faith and optimism that he could prevail in the end regardless of the difficulties, and, at the same time, be willing to confront the most brutal facts of his current situation, whatever they may be. This pairing of unbridled optimism with the acknowledgement that your situation is brutal is now known as the *Stockdale Paradox.*

H aving Fun

When we face the fearsome KILLER 'B's, we will often need to confront their brutality with optimism and a fun-loving demeanor. Here are several ideas on how to incorporate fun, humor, laughter and play in this battle.

Work Hard at Play

> "Smart people have trouble learning because it involves so much floundering in failure. Play is hard work."
> Chris Argyris

In the first chapter on Implementing Your 'A's (*Believe That You Can Change*), I discussed the stunning power of neuroplasticity, the ability of the brain to grow and develop. The same can be said about the importance of **play**. As you go about the hard work of learning how to Thrive, it is critical to remember to play. And here's why.

Play engages the prefrontal cortex (the most highly evolved brain area), which nourishes our highest-level cognitive functions — including those related to mental imagery, self-knowledge and memory. In other words, play provides the "emotional fuel" which promotes discovery and learning.

Some of our most brilliant thinkers knew the importance of play in helping us improve our ability to reason and better understand the world. Einstein, for example, credited his development of the theory of relativity in part to his ability to create a child-like fantasy world. This is probably why he came to his famous conclusion that "imagination is more important than knowledge."

Play, therefore, should not just be considered kids' stuff. It is interesting to note that in environments that stifle play, brainpower may actually decrease as it does in children with failure-to-thrive syndrome.

When it comes to THRIVING in our adult life, it is important to learn how to play. Playfulness, humor and fun are important tools in knowing how to effectively attack KILLER 'B's.

Laughing All the Way!

"If you bottled it [laughter] all up in a pill, you'd need FDA approval."
Dr. Lee Berk, laughter researcher

Laughter is no joke! Until quite recently, however, laughter was not thought of as being therapeutic. But that started to change with the popularity of Norman Cousins' *Anatomy of an Illness*. In this book he credits humor and laughter with aiding his recovery from a serious illness.

Since the publication of Cousins' book, laughter has been subjected to a number of carefully controlled scientific studies. The results — laughter boosts the body's immune system by releasing beneficial hormones which decrease the stress hormones that can lead to disease. Research also suggests that laughter can lower blood pressure, be aerobic for the heart and elevate moods by increasing levels of serotonin.

One physician highly influenced by this research on laughter was Dr. Madan Kataria from Mumbai, India. In 1995 Dr. Kataria, now known as the father of laughing yoga, decided to field-test the impact of laughter on himself. Along with four other people he started a "Laughter Club." Quickly the number of participants grew, and today there is a worldwide movement of over 6,000 clubs in more than 60 countries.

One of the early breakthroughs in his new-found technology of "laughing without jokes" was the scientific research which showed the human mind doesn't know how to make a distinction between fake and genuine laughter — either way it produces happy chemistry. With that, the concept of "laughing for no reason" was born. When Dr. Kataria's wife brought in her experience as a yoga teacher and suggested adding deep yoga breathing to the laughter routine, the "Laughter Yoga" technique was launched and trademarked.

All this "happy talk" about fun, humor and laughter is a deadly serious attempt to help you find an effective way to thrive when faced with KILLER 'B's. Making it fun can be one of the techniques most effective in disarming the 'B's, whether they are the subtle slayers (the killing me softly types!) or the fear-provoking ferocious types.

S uccess Stories

Once again (!) we have talked a lot about theory and concepts. Now it is time to hear the success stories of several individuals who have put theory into practice. The following three people have implemented 'A' activities by attacking KILLER 'B's, whether subtle or fearsome, and have actively developed ways to make the process fun and enjoyable.

First, Cousin Dave's story. Dave is a hard-working and successful musician, but he had never produced that breakthrough 'A' album. The culprits holding him back were those pesky, subtle *Killer* 'B's. Once identified, he took action.

In his own words, this is his story.

Dave's Story

> *"I don't want to be a woulda', coulda', shoulda' kind of guy. I'd rather go for it."*
> Jon Bon Jovi (from a *60 Minutes* interview)

The image of musicians is often that of being carefree, "too cool for school," or even flaky. That stereotype might be true for some rock artists, but it does not speak to the life of this everyday working musician. I have always been the kind of responsible, hard-working musician who feels the importance of providing for my family. I have always been a survivor, willing to take jobs that I really didn't want to do. Those 'B' gigs made me feel like I had accomplished something and kept food on the table. The only problem is that I was surviving and not thriving.

It is true that even the most successful musicians will take gigs that are not perfect just to pay the bills. But what I now realize is that I was not spending enough time working toward becoming what I pictured as a teenager. As a composer and music producer, I always wanted to be like Henry Mancini or Quincy Jones. I was hoping that someone along the way would recognize my talents and give me the gig of a lifetime! That could happen, but you can bet that Henry and Quincy honed in on their goals like a laser beam. A little luck probably helped, but there is no doubt that they were both dedicated and focused on their dream. Likewise, I am highly goal oriented and good at what I do. But, I realized a higher truth,

"Dreams don't come true by slaving away at 'B' projects."

A year or so ago, I had the opportunity to create a solo album. The album could be whatever I wanted it to be. The offer was made by a long time client as a gift. He would pay for it, and market it. Wow, what an offer! But, of course, being the practical, responsible person that I am, my first thought was to do something "safe." Since I didn't really have "name" recognition, I thought maybe if I did an album of movie themes, or Beatles songs that I would have a chance of selling some copies. I was willing to do something like that, but ... my heart wasn't in it.

During one of many fun and interesting conversations with Cousin Alan (author of this book), he asked me, "What would you *really* like this project to be?" I said in sort of a shy way, "Well, there is this big band that I know. They are very popular in the jazz world right now, and I would love to be the featured artist with that band." I have known the leader for a long time, but it seems like a total long shot that I could accomplish such a thing. Alan replied by saying, "That's what you need to do!" I said, "I don't know, he may not be receptive to the idea and I don't even know if it's something that could be marketable." I was making every excuse in the world to not pick up the phone and find out if it could be a possibility. Alan said, "I'm going to see you in a few weeks, and before that time I want you to make this happen. It's not an option!!" Well, he is older than me, and I've always looked up to him, so I said, "Okay, I promise."

Later that week I reluctantly picked up the phone and called the band leader. Like many musicians and artistic people, I hate to be rejected. Because it is crushing and demoralizing, I sometimes don't even ask. It seems easier to never do it than be turned down. Well, to my surprise and delight, he said, "Yes, that sounds like a great idea."

We proceeded with the project and in several months we had a smashing public debut of the album. It has already received many glowing reviews by jazz publications. I have no idea how successful it will be in the long run, but I can say this with certainty:

≈ I have finally done something for me; and

≈ **This is the best work I have ever done.**

Even if it is not a huge hit, it is something that I am proud of and something that will take me closer to my teenage dreams. At the very least, it has confirmed that I need to continue pursuing my 'A' list activities and become a "card-carrying" THRIVER!

The second success story involves Jeff, now a highly successful entertainment lawyer in New York City. He was raised in a family of fear; danger lurked around every corner! But look what happened when we instituted a "Swashbuckler Program," where we mocked and scoffed at the fear-provoking KILLER 'B's that stifled his 'A' activities.

Jeff's Story

"Don't let the fear of striking out get in your way."
Babe Ruth

My road to becoming a swashbuckler began by simply pretending to be one. And, by stringing together many swashbuckling-type experiences over a 20-year period, I "suddenly" realized that I was not just swashbuckling, I WAS a swashbuckler. This for someone who was a painfully shy, non-risk type of guy!

The lesson learned: break down difficult-to-do experiences to their smallest building blocks, and accept that they will be scary but you can get through enough of them to start making a real difference in your life that will allow you to live life more fully.

One of the early and important experiences occurred when I was 22 years old. I had just joined the West L.A. "Y" in Los Angeles. While doing a Yoga-type headstand against a wall, a beautiful young woman asked if I was uncomfortable holding the headstand position for so long (she later revealed that she thought by standing upside-down near her that I was trying to attract her attention, which actually was not true)... Thus began the first conversation with my future wife, with me speaking to her upside-down!

Well, at some point I righted myself and continued the conversation. After a few minutes of chit-chat, during which I was way too scared to ask her for a date or her phone number, she simply said good-bye and left. For the next few minutes I sat there, rationalizing how bold I was to have spoken to such a beautiful girl (even though she had initiated the discussion), and how surely in the future we would run into each other again, and that at some point I would have the guts to ask her out.

Then reality set in. I might never see her again, and I had blown a golden opportunity. And worst of all, I knew deep down that I had simply chickened out.

Well, I reluctantly finished my workout, hit the showers and was just about to leave the building when I noticed that she was teaching an aerobics class. I stopped to look through the glass door at the class. She was at the front of the room with her back to me. Then a miracle happened. She turned her head, saw me, smiled and waved, and then went back to teach.

I headed out the door, intoxicated by the wave I had received. As I headed home, I fantasized about the next time I would run into her at the Y and how I would ask her out then. It was comforting to know that such a day would come. Or would it? ... Once home, I thought about all the missed opportunities I had experienced with girls over the years. Then I decided that I needed to prove to myself that I could do something immediate to capitalize on this just-missed opportunity.

Yikes! I suddenly got hit with a wave of terror just at the thought that I would even attempt something so rash. But once that wave passed, I was hit by a wave of self-loathing. I had to do something to meet this girl. Knowing her first name (I at least had gotten THAT information), I figured that I could call her at the Y, and either get her on the phone or leave her a message. It was an excellent plan. So simple, yet I was absolutely TERRIFIED to execute it.

I had been in therapy for a while with Alan Hedman, who had introduced to me the concept of doing things that were emotionally scary, but highly important nonetheless. I was beginning to learn that in some ways scary experiences are important simply BECAUSE they are scary. Alan told me that in life it was crucial to recognize that fear wouldn't necessarily go away during certain experiences, and that we should "feel the fear and do it anyway."

So I said to myself, "ok, you can pick up the telephone, can't you?" And my Self said, "yes I can, I can at least do that," and I did so. And I just sat there and listened to the dial tone for a minute or so, and then hung up the phone in panic. Regrouping, I picked it back up again, and repeated this hanging up silliness a few more times. Then I said to myself (with the phone at my ear, dial tone mocking me), "ok, you can push a few buttons on this piece of plastic, no?" And my Self said "yes I can," and I did so. I pushed those seven buttons that constituted the numbers that would link me with the Y. That much I could do.

Before I knew it, someone answered the line. Fighting through the terror to simply hang up, I asked if I could speak with "X," the young woman who had probably just finished teaching her last aerobics class. I was then put on hold. I was on hold for perhaps a minute or so, but it felt interminable. I really wanted to hang up, to go to the bathroom and pee (yeah, at this point I really had to pee badly). And I even heard my heart pounding in my chest, as my breathing got shallow. The only thing preventing me from slamming the phone down was the grave intuition that if I did, I'd loathe myself forever.

"Hello?" a bright, adorable voice chirped at the other end of the line. "Hi," I responded. "Um, this is Jeff, the guy who was talking to you while I was upside down a little while ago." The response came back, "Oh hi!, how are you?" Unable (i.e. too scared) to make any small talk, it just came right out of me: "Well, I thought that maybe you'd like to grab dinner sometime."

And we did. And I will tell you something — the experience that afternoon of having taken a risk and landing a date with that girl, in what at the time felt like such a bold maneuver, gave me tremendous confidence during the date and in future experiences. Experiences that started building upon themselves.

I am now 47 years old, and look back at my West L.A. Y experience as an initial building-block on my road to becoming a swashbuckler. Over the years, I drew on that experience and had many more experiences in which I took emotional risks and really aimed for things that I wanted.

I've played the piano in front of hundreds of people, been interviewed on live television, sought out supermodels as clients (I'm an entertainment lawyer), argued with dour and powerful judges, said things to family, spouses and children that needed to be said. As a result, I have attained a certain equanimity in the world and peace within myself because I've had many, many tough experiences that I got through with the "swashbuckler" mentality.

Now when people really get to know me, they are surprised to learn how painfully shy I was, and how long it took me to develop self-confidence, quality relationships and a modicum of success in the world. Now I AM a swashbuckler and people think of me in that light. Little do they know that the frightened little boy is still inside me, egging me on to conquer my fears and live life to the fullest.

This third segment is about a school that was already high-functioning and a headmaster who wanted to see his school become the very best. It's a story on how he guided the process of making a fundamental culture change in human development; an 'A' success story about an organization, not just an individual.

The Headmaster's Story

"Have the courage of your own authenticity rather than being a master imitator."
Peter Bachmann, Headmaster @ Flintridge Prep

When I first became head of a school, I was a master imitator. I dutifully read all of the requisite books and articles, took pages of notes at conferences with sages, and became great at implementing other people's ideas. After five years, I could look back in pride at a school's leap forward by any conventional benchmarks. But slowly, I noticed my increasing boredom while I sat studiously at those conferences, until one day, I recalled a great teacher of my youth listening to a debate about the American Presidency, until he finally asked: "Do we need a president?"

The freedom of the question imploded in my head; the ultimate fresh, radical perspective of starting without assumptions. The implosion forced a series of questions: why should our school follow another's vision, rather than strike out originally on its own? Why shouldn't I define my headship personally and idiosyncratically? Perhaps I'd have more fun leading the conference discussion rather than sitting politely listening.

And so, like Huck Finn, we "lit out for the territory." We developed a human development program that was seamless and organic to our school's culture. We hired eccentric geniuses and invited their creativity; and after several years, we became the school that other schools visited. Our chief advice to them: grow your crops out of your own unique soil. Have the courage of your own authenticity.

Turns out, school is more fun that way.

Now, if you REALLY want to implement your 'A's, you will have to learn how to "wince." Creating a crisis while surrounding yourself with inspirational thoughts and ideas is the subject of our next chapter.

Nope — nothing on this page.

Create a Crisis

Man cannot discover new oceans unless he
has the courage to lose sight of the shore.

Motto from the KEMTAH company

In our final chapter we'd like to leave you
with a little more knowledge and a dose of
inspiration. The knowledge will come
in the discussion of the crisis/change
dynamic, while the big finale will
include inspirational prose, poetry
and quotations.

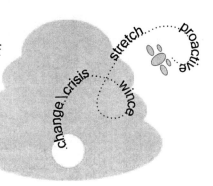

D ynamics of Change and Crisis

"Crisis is an opportunity for change."
Chinese proverb

Implementing Your 'A's involves CHANGE, and change ultimately involves CRISIS. Crisis, in turn, requires MORE CHANGE which inevitably

creates MORE CRISIS. You can't get away from it — change and crisis are inexorably tied together.

Implementing Your 'A's also involves searching for "stretch goals," making sure those goals make you "wince," and having a tough love team for support and challenge. Years ago I developed the following model to describe the dynamics of change and crisis, and how to implement decision-making that results in 'A' level activity.

Decision-Making Model for Risk-Takers

"Life is either a daring adventure or it is nothing."
Helen Keller

Stretch Goal

The Question:	Is the goal a little outside my comfort zone?
The Plan:	Need to do the necessary homework and research
	Use the S-M-A-R-T Goals method for action steps

Wince Factor

The Question: Does this goal make me and/or others a bit uncomfortable?

The Plan: Use a gut check to test the comfort level
                  Challenge yourself but don't hurt yourself; i.e. no self-sabotage

Tough Love Team

The Question: Do I have a team that will support and prod me to reach this goal?

The Plan: Choose team members who are advisory, not managerial
                  Team members must be able to apply "tough love"

To get a deeper understanding of the dynamics of change/crisis and decision-making, let's do a quick psychodynamic/cognitive behavioral analysis. I know ... a bit on the academic side ... but I can't help myself.
CHANGE/CRISIS AND DECISION-MAKING CAN BE:

Externally Generated OR Internally Generated;

Unconscious OR Conscious;

Reactive OR Proactive.

Here's how it works:

Generally speaking, Externally Generated + Unconscious + Reactive = **SURVIVING**. In this modality, you are not in charge of your own life.

Rather, you are waiting for your lucky day or for something magical to happen. This can be a very long wait. As a Chinese proverb says, "Man who sit on chair with mouth open wait very long time for roast duck to fly in."

On the other hand, Internally Generated + Conscious + Proactive = THRIV-ING. This is when you feel as though you are in charge of your own life and destiny. In this situation, you see yourself as the captain of your ship.

A hypothetical example may help: You can voluntarily leave your job in order to move on to something more challenging (internally generated), OR, you can wait to be fired (externally generated). The reasons for leaving can be clearly understood (conscious) OR very murky (unconscious). And, you can take action by your initiation (proactive) OR by waiting till "something comes along" before making a reactive decision.

I am a strong proponent of *Creating a Crisis* in decision-making (maybe you already figured that out by the title of this chapter!). My suggestion would be to *internally generate* a crisis by leaving that low-challenging job, moving to a new location that revives your spirit, and/or deciding to write a book, etc. Consciously, "know thyself" well enough to understand that your decision is 'A' level — it is the "song in your heart." And finally, be proactive by initiating and implementing your 'A' Plan with the help of your tough love team.

An inventive way to "create a crisis" was conducted by the same school described in the previous chapter. Students in the Psychology class were given the following assignment:

Think of something that you fear the most and do it

or

Take the opportunity to try something you've always wanted to do.

Our very own Madison Z., a primary editor for this book, took advantage of this assignment by trying something she found terrifying.

Practical Application:
Psychology Class "Stretching Yourself" Projects

"Do the thing we fear and death of fear is certain."
Ralph Waldo Emerson

Madison Z's weekend church retreat

My "stretch" project involved going on a church retreat over a three-day weekend. While this might seem normal to some people, I was terrified because I had no religious upbringing. I had always been curious about religion and wanted to learn more about Christianity, but at the same time I was scared. My biggest fears were being judged by others, being looked down upon for not being Christian, standing out as an "other," and simply the unfamiliarity of it all: not knowing the worship songs, praying out loud, conducting bible studies, etc. However, I knew that this fear was a sign that the experience might be one to grow from.

I learned a lot about Christianity in general, but perhaps more importantly I learned that it's okay — even good — to ask questions, and that I didn't have to be afraid to ask. Also, I realized that if you're open-minded, even when in an uncomfortable situation, you can gain a lot from any experience and have fun as well!

NOTE: For three more interesting examples of students doing something fearful, check out the addendum at the end of this chapter.

nspirational Prose, Poetry and Quotations

And now for the big finale, selected writings that will absolutely, positively inspire you to take action! I know that's not very subtle, but this section is designed to help you learn more about the the crisis/change dynamic AND to inspire you in your 'A' journey. The first portion (prose) features several authors who share their insights about change and crisis. In the poetry segment, we will share some excerpts from Roger Housden's *Ten Poems to Change Your Life*. Lastly, a smorgasbord of quotations that are pithy and memorable.

Prose

"Dare to be honest with yourself."
Po Bronson

Po Bronson (*What Should I Do With My Life*) interviewed a vast number of ordinary (read *real*) people who "dared to be honest with themselves" on a journey to discover in themselves gifts they rarely realized they had. He learned that it was in hard times that people usually changed the course of their life; in good times, they frequently only talked about change.

These themes evolved from his interviews:

≈ Change is not easy / It's not supposed to be easy;

≈ Most people make mistakes / Most people have to learn the hardest lessons more than once.

For me, Bronson's most insightful and inspirational contribution was his discussion on how our fears can turn to misconceptions that prevent us from realizing our 'A's. Here's how he describes it:

> "But we also have many psychological stumbling blocks that keep us from finding ourselves. Some of these are badly tangled **misconceptions**, some are deeply rooted **fears**. The two are related — like any prejudice, misconceptions get fabricated and sustained by fears. These psychological stumbling blocks are often less real than we imagine. By confronting them, we begin to see around all our obstacles, even the seemingly insurmountable ones. If you take care of these obstacles, you create an environment where the truth is invited into your life."
> [emphasis mine]

The inspirational **gem** to remember: by honestly confronting our fears and misconceptions, we can render our KILLER 'B's helpless. Remember, 'B's are like ghosts, only able to survive by feeding on our fears. Honest confrontation with these fears will allow us to realize our 'A's.

Naomi Levy (*To Begin Again*) reminds us of the price we have to pay when we set out to transform our lives. Well-meaning people may tell us about the huge mistake we are making. This criticism can make it difficult to overcome self-doubt when we are taking such huge risks with our future. In addition to the criticism from those closest to us, there may be even a higher price to pay in realizing our dreams:

"Sometimes the price we must pay when we set out to fulfill our longings is not just criticism; we may have to face shame and gossip or even the possibility of being ostracized from our own community. The cost of realizing our dreams may be high, but the rewards are immeasurable."

The **gem** to remember: the rewards of realizing our dreams are immeasurable. It's just like the MasterCard commercial says (with slight modifications!): the cost of the hard steps you have to take is X $, and yet the final result of living your 'A' dream is priceless.

The final inspiration from Prose is more practical. Jeanne Segal (*The Language of Emotional Intelligence*) outlines how to prepare for change. She outlines some steps to take, and in parentheses are my own editorial comments.

Start by observing what gets in the way.
(Get to know your personal KILLER 'B's 'up close and personal'.)

Carve out some quality time for acquiring new skills.
(Take time to muse.)

Motivate yourself every day.
(Seriously listen to your dreams.)
(Constantly experience the passion of vision and the power of goals.)

Be prepared for setbacks.
(Have fun; realize that you'll make lots of mistakes and that you'll not let any roadblocks stop you from pursuing your 'A's.)

Reward yourself.
(Take time to notice and appreciate your hard work and the positive

changes your are making.)

Don't attempt change without the help and support of others.
(Surround yourself with other 'A's and make sure you have a tough love team.)

The **gem**: a step-by-step and practical outline for implementing your desired changes.

Poetry

"*Good poetry has the power to start a fire in your life.*"
Roger Housden

Many of you already know how the power of poetry can inspire you to change. I must admit to being a late (but enthusiastic) convert. Part of this conversion occurred when a client gave me a copy of Roger Housden's *Ten Poems to Change Your Life*.

In his introduction, Housden proclaims that reading poetry can be rigorous, demanding and ecstatic. And it can be a dangerous practice: dangerous because you may never be the same again! He then quotes from the eminent American poet, Emily Dickinson, who described the reading of poetry in this way:

"*If I read a book and it makes my whole body so cold no fire can warm me, I know that is poetry. If I feel physically as if the top of my head were taken off, I know that is poetry. These are the only ways I know it. Is there any other way?*"

I would like to share excerpts from two poems in Housden's book — *The Journey* by Mary Oliver and *Zero Circle* by Rumi, a thirteenth-century Persian mystic.

The Journey
by Mary Oliver

One day you finally knew
what you had to do, and began,
though the voices around you
kept shouting
their bad advice...

But you didn't stop.
You knew what you had to do...

It was already late enough...
But little by little,
as you left their voices behind...
there was a new voice
which you ...
recognized as your own,
that kept you company...
determined to do
the only thing you could do —
determined to save
the only life that you could save.

Housden reports that even after hundreds of readings, this poem still "grabs me by the shoulders, shakes me hard, and demands I look again at how honestly I am living my life."

This poem grabbed me too, because it so eloquently describes the major themes of this book. For example, we may desperately want to make changes in our life, but the KILLER 'B's are relentless in trying to prevent us from realizing our dreams. But when we find our own voice and live our 'A' life, we will save the only life we have and "not go to the grave with the song still in us."

Zero Circle
by Rumi

And now for a little Rumi. As a result of many contemporary translators, Rumi has recently become one of the bestselling poets in America. Listen to the beginning of this poem from *Zero Circle* and see if it inspires you.

Be helpless, dumbfounded,
Unable to say yes or no.
Then a stretcher will come from grace
to gather us up.

I love the image Rumi uses of a stretcher (our tough love supporters) coming in grace to gather us up when we feel weak and helpless. And, with the help of our stretchers, we will be able to be lifted up in our 'A' journey.

As I admitted earlier, I am a recent convert to poetry and have a limited repertoire from which to draw upon. But it appears to me that poetry can provide a rich reservoir for all of us in our quest to find the inspiration to change.

And now, to an old favorite — quotations!

Quotations

> *"You can never have too many thought-provoking quotes in a book!"*
> Alan Hedman

I have deliberately and liberally used quotes throughout this book because I find them particularly pungent and memorable. In fact, the first on the following list was pivotal in helping me make a commitment to several difficult 'A' decisions.

With any or all of the quotes included, you are invited to use them for inspiration. Put your favorites in a place where you will see them on a regular basis. Pin them to your clothing, your bathroom mirror, your forehead, anywhere you'll have them as a constant reminder!

Although these quotes do no fit into neat categories, you will notice that many are designed to inspire us to "get started," while others seem to remind us to "keep it going" when the going gets tough.

Enjoy!

> *"Jump and build your parachute on the way down."*

or, the gentler Swedish version,

> *"Jump and your wings will appear."*

"We must suffer from one of two pains, the pain of discipline or the pain of regret. The difference is, discipline weighs ounces while regret weighs tons."
Jim Rohn

"Even eagles need a push."

"Not to decide is to decide."
Harvey Cox

"Action is the antidote to despair."
Joan Baez

"And then the day came when the risk to remain tight in a bud was more painful than the risk it took to blossom."
Anais Nin

"Dream as if you will live forever; live as if you will die tomorrow."

"Dreams are the touchstones of our character."
Henry David Thoreau

"Every truly great accomplishment is at first impossible."
Chinese proverb

"If you want to walk on the water, you have to get out of the boat."
John Ortberg

"Be wrong rather than being afraid."

"If you lay down with dogs, you'll pick up fleas."
East Texas saying

"Mistakes — the building blocks of success; taking risks takes you forward."

"People are always blaming their circumstances for what they are. I don't believe in circumstances. The people who get on in this world are the people who get up and look for the circumstances they want, and if they can't find them, make them."
George Bernard Shaw

"There are two good times to plant a tree; 30 years ago and today."

"If you are not living on the edge, you're taking up too much space."
Helen Keller

"A ship in a harbor is safe but that is not what ships were built for.."
John Shedd

"Catch the trade winds in your sails. Explore. Dream. Discover."
Mark Twain

"A fool with a plan can outsmart a genius with no plan."
T. Boone Pickens

"I don't regret what I've done, I only regret what I haven't done."

"You miss 100% of the shots you don't take."
Wayne Gretzky, hockey great

"There is a wisdom in the waves, high born and beautiful, for those who would only paddle out. The waves will come to you, just paddle out. And you'll catch one. The only way to fail is if you just sit on the beach. Sitting on the beach is the greatest sin of all. You must paddle out."
Motto in surfing

I hope the prose, poetry and quotations have summarized some of the major principles necessary for "Implementing Your 'A's", and can serve as inspiration when your motivation wavers.

In the final section of the book, I have included ideas and action steps you can take to truly put *THRIVING* into practice. In the Workbook and Discovery Guide, please feel free to use any or all parts that you find useful.

As Roy Rogers said to "me" as a kid:

"Happy Trails to You!"
(in your pursuit of *THRIVING*)

ddendum

Practical Application:
Psychology Class "Stretching Yourself" Projects

Mika and her vegan caper

Mika decided to go vegan for two weeks by avoiding meat, dairy, and any other animal byproducts. This was a "stretch" for her because she described herself as a meat and food lover in general who never before had restrictions on her diet. And, she had always been adventurous with food. Thus, she created a crisis by limiting herself.

Her biggest fears? A loss of energy and gaining weight from eating a lot of carbohydrates. During that dieting period, Mika was pleasantly surprised to learn that vegans still have a lot of options in terms of food. Although it was increasingly hard to discipline herself, especially when others were stuffing their faces with meat in front of her, she had the strength to stick to her plan and as a result felt accomplished.

Karina goes "makeupless" for two weeks

Karina opted to go two weeks without wearing makeup. She chose this to see if she could give up something that had become a daily habit, and then to see how it would affect both others' opinions of her and her own self-concept. She was mostly scared of being self-conscious and worried that people would laugh at her or judge her.

In the beginning, it was hard because of the dramatic and sudden change. She admitted that she had previously used makeup as a mask, an answer to her problems if she felt sad or tired. However, the experience changed how she perceived herself — in a good way! Karina realized she didn't need makeup. To help her gain the most from her experience, she also kept a journal during the project.

Effie nails a role in the senior play

Effie always had an aspiration to be in a high school play, but had "never gotten around to it." When the second semester of senior year rolled around, she decided it was time to take advantage of the opportunity.

Her greatest fear was based on her nervousness of how others would perceive her. She was afraid people would think she was being disingenuous by taking a step outside what she was usually known for (good student, musician). Another fear was that she would mess up, almost to the point of thinking she "shouldn't" be in a play. She also felt out of place and was intimidated being around more accomplished actors.

She had some wonderful learnings! Nobody is perfect! Everyone forgets lines here and there and makes mistakes — even the most seasoned actors and actresses. Rehearsals were not as bad as she thought they would be. She liked making people laugh; sometimes the funniest moments, she realized, are random and unplanned. Although she is not 100% over her fear, being in a play was a good first step outside her comfort zone, AND, it was really a fun experience.

Section Five
Workbook &
Discovery Guide

"I hear..............................and I forget;
I see................................and I remember;
I do.................................and I understand."
Chinese Proverb

KILLER B'S & WORKER B'S is designed to help you "hear" and "see" many things about Survivng and THRIVING, but reading alone is not sufficient for achieving your dream. Much of what we read will unfortunately be quickly forgotten. We are shooting for something higher — *understanding*. We want THRIVING to become part of your DNA. This will only happen by *doing*.

REMINDER: Please feel free to use any or all of the ideas, suggestions, and exercises that you find meaningful and useful. If something is not relevant to you, move on! ... Also, for those areas that you find particularly helpful, we highly recommend the use of a separate notebook in which to write more extensively.

This Workbook will include a brief recap of the main ideas in each chapter, followed by questions, exercises and/or suggested action steps that will help you understand the principles presented.

ENJOY!

WARM-UP

Understanding Your Choices / Key Players & Key Principles

SHORT SUMMARY: We tried to summarize one of the the key questions of life as a simple choice of whether to survive or thrive. And, if you truly have "a song in your heart," acknowledging and dealing with your KILLER 'B's is critical.

Let's review some basics:

➡ Do you have a dream for your life or a significant aspect of your life? If so, write it down (when you do, the power of writing will become apparent). How did you come to this dream? Feel free to use words or pictures to describe this dream.

_____

_____

_____

➡ What is your present baseline and what is your goal for the future; that is, using the description below, circle the choice which most accurately describes where you are at the present time and where you would like to be in the future.

NOW	A/A-	B+	B	B-	C
	Full-on thriving or thriving most of the time	Getting close but not quite there	A true-blue Worker 'B'	Worker 'B'; could go either way	Life isn't so great
FUTURE	A/A-	B+	B	B-	C

➡ What are some of the best things that could happen for you by reading this book and doing the suggested exercises in the Workbook & Discovery Guide?

_____

_____

_____

_____

_____

_____

_____

PRIMER ON 'A's & 'B's

Thoughts from the Experts

SHORT SUMMARY: If you thought the idea of *THRIVING* sounded pretty good, it seemed wise to share what "experts" have to say about it! This overview included some scholarly, philosophical and religious ideas as well as some "fun" thoughts.

Here are some issues to consider:

➡ What did you learn about the basis for happiness and fulfillment (flow) from Csikszentmihalyi? (see page 16) How does it relate to your life?

➡ Bronson interviewed "real" people who "dared to be honest with themselves." How would you describe your readiness to honestly assess the question of "what should you do with your life?"

➡ What were the most valuable insights you gained from Kushner and Tolstoy (see page 20 and page 21) about living a fulfilling life?

➡ If you don't already own a copy of *Jonathan Livingston Seagull,* are you going to run out and buy a copy after reading this short review?! ... Are you a "good gull" doing mainly what you should, or do you want to be really good at what you could be or do?

➡ Many other authors not included here have written thoughtful works on *THRIVING.* Who do you find particularly insightful and inspiring? Give some examples.

Distinction Between 'A's & 'B's

SHORT SUMMARY: This chapter was designed to help you distinguish between your urgent and important activities. Learning the difference between your *KILLER* 'B' behaviors and your *THRIVING* 'A' activities was described as key to charting the path toward living your dream.

Try the following activities

➡ Take a look at Covey's Time Management Matrix (see page 24). Honestly ask yourself several questions:

Do you find yourself consumed by urgent matters (Q 1 and Q 3)? List several "favorites."

Q 3 is called the "quadrant of deception." Can you think of some of your critical activities which are based primarily on the priorities of others rather than your own? Examples:

Overall, how comfortable are you living in Q 2, the "quadrant of quality?"

➡ Joseph's Story (see page 29) illustrates the importance of imagining how you will feel AFTER taking an 'A' action. Apply his thought process to one of your potential 'A' activities. Outline what it could look like.

➡ For a truly revealing exercise, keep a log of your 'A' and 'B' activities for two weeks. Summarize what you learned.

The Power of *KILLER* 'B's

SHORT SUMMARY: *KILLER* 'B's were the real black hat villains in our story. In this chapter we described several of the most potent and destructive 'B's.

This is analysis and introspection time; please address the following questions.

➡ Was the reference to Jeff Foxworthy's "redneck humor" useful? Please underline one of the following:

   ≈   Vital to my understanding of *KILLER* 'B's

   ≈   Silly and unnecessary

Hint — you will score points with the author if you choose vital…

➡ Are you crystal clear on your plan for implementing your most important goals in life? Describe your plan, as clearly and concisely as possible.

➡ Do you qualify as one of the "nice people" in the world? If so, can you see ways that you have suspended your 'A' agenda because you were unable to say no to others? Give examples:

➡ Are you plagued by busyness, the "shoulds" and responsibilities in your life? Where do these "shoulds" (often KILLER 'B's) and "wants" (your 'A' agenda) usually collide? Describe:

➡ Describe the three most powerful KILLER 'B's in your life:

Numero uno: Fear of failing and not being happy.

Numero dos: Constant worry about my health e.g. Passing out

Numero tres: Constant worrying about what I'm going to do w/ my life.

Why So Many WORKER 'B's?

SHORT SUMMARY: We outlined some of the obvious and conscious reasons for the paucity of 'A's as well as some that were less obvious and probably unconscious.

Get ready for more personal analysis and introspection.

➡ Would you consider yourself someone who has settled into doing 'B' activities? What are some of your "favorite" settling activities?

➡ So, did you like the Pickle Theory?! (see page 38) On my website (www. dralanhedman.com) it's one of the favorite choices. What is your rating of the theory?

GREAT	Okay, but hardly great	A waste of perfectly good ink

➡ How do you and hard work get along? Can you work long and hard in a regular, consistent farmer-like way? Give some examples of personal hard work that would make a farmer proud, and/or some ways in which you found it difficult to be persistent and steady?

_____

_____

➡ Do you truly believe that you are 'A' material? Can you embrace the idea of selfishness (as I defined it) and make it your goal? At the present time, do your priorities receive sufficient allocation to match your vision? Take the time to honestly analyze yourself; describe what you learn.

_____

_____

➡ Fear of success is a relatively new concept in psychological literature. And, it probably explains why many people are 'A'-aversive. If you are truly committed to becoming a THRIVING 'A,' paint a picture of yourself as strong, humble AND successful.

_____

_____

You Deserve to be an 'A'

SHORT SUMMARY: In this cheerleading portion of our story, you were challenged to believe that you have the "perfect right" to be an 'A'. Jesus, Jimmy Carter and a host of other 'A's gave examples from which to live and learn.

Check out your belief system and the type of person you would like to emulate.

➡ Overall, in your present state, how would you best describe yourself?

Non-assertive | Aggressive | Assertive

If you are not assertive, what are some ways in which you can learn to be?

....

....

....

➡ Ask yourself the "Jimmy Carter question" — why not the best? How do you stack up? Are others seeing the best possible 'you'? Describe how you are at your best and where you'd like to improve.

....

....

....

....

➡ Did you know that Jesus believes we deserve to be 'A's?! How would you assess your own talent level and how you are using your talents?

_____

_____

_____

➡ List five of your 'A' List 'A's, and why you chose them.

_____

_____

_____

_____

➡ Which of the Quiet 'A's inspired you? If you are more of the quiet 'A' type, write the memorial you would like written about yourself.

_____

_____

_____

_____

'A's **Trump** 'B's

SHORT SUMMARY: We talked about how *THRIVING* 'A' activities have some built-in qualities that allow them to "trump" *KILLER* 'B' behavior. These included the passion of vision, the power of boldness and the fact that it's "hard to go back" (once you've experienced 'A's).

It's time to see how your 'A's can trump the 'B's.

➡ Remember a time when you were so passionate about a decision that no thing or no body could stop you. What was the vision? Why were you so passionate about it? Describe yourself at that unstoppable best!

_____

_____

_____

_____

➡ Take time to re-experience the power of **boldness**. Use the following simple formula to create another situation where you will make a bold decision:

Your bold thought
_____

Your brave first step
_____

Visualize what genius, power and magic you will experience
_____

➡ Look to the future in your life; what can you envision yourself being or doing that would make it hard to go back to your old way of living? Complete the following statements:

When I _____it will be hard

to_____

After I've developed_____I will no longer

want to_____

In spending time with_____I will probably

spend less time with_____

DISCOVERING YOUR 'A'S

Seriously Listen to Your Dreams

SHORT SUMMARY: Seriously listening to your dreams, literal or metaphorical, was presented as a profound way to discover your personal 'A' dream in life.

➡ Think about the dreams you have experienced in your life. Have you experienced a dream that gave you insight about a challenge or dangerous situation you were facing? Describe what you learned.

➡ Dreams have been described as "windows to your soul." What have your dreams told you about the bold steps you need to take in order to mobilize action toward implementing your goals?

➡ Okay, get serious about listening to your dreams. You've had dreams which give you some profound insights about your life. Describe some aspects of a dream that really "rocked your world." What was the message? What are you doing about listening to the message in those dreams?

Make Use of Jealousy and Envy

SHORT SUMMARY: Jealousy and envy were discussed as often over-looked tools for helping us discover our 'A's. These emotions pointed us toward activities we really want to do, reminded us that we are not doing them, and provided realistic stretch goals.

➡ What do you think about the idea of viewing jealousy as something useful and powerful in discovering your 'A's?

What a profound idea	Never thought about it, but could be useful	Not buying it

➡ **Projection** is often unconscious and therefore hard to recognize in yourself. But, can you think of an attribute that you ascribe to someone else which also belongs to you? How can this awareness be useful to you?

➡ Think about the *"shoulds"* and *"wants"* in your life. Make a list of each to see what you discover about yourself.

Shoulds   # Wants

I should...   *I want...*

_____   _____

_____   _____

_____   _____

_____   _____

_____   _____

_____   _____

_____   _____

_____   _____

Which were the easiest to list? Were you able to describe any "wants" that identify 'A' activities that could be in your life? Do you also notice some *KILLER* 'B's (probably "shoulds") that need to be eliminated or neutralized?

_____

_____

_____

_____

➡ Carefully analyze yourself to see if there is a person that causes you to be jealous. Are they doing something that you really want to do? Can you see how this might be a way of discovering an unknown or hidden personal 'A'? Describe what you learn from this self-analysis.

Listen to Your Body/Listen to Your Soul

SHORT SUMMARY: Listening to our body and to our soul helped us discover what to embrace (the sweet spot) and what to reject or repulse (the bitter spot) in the pursuit of our dreams.

➡ The "sweet spot" is a beautiful and useful concept for discovering our 'A's. Can you identify those times in sports, art or music, or in some other aspect of your life where you were in "flow"? Describe what it felt like. What does it tell you about discovering your true calling in life?

➡ Identifying a "bitter spot" in your life can help you discover something that is not an 'A' activity. Visualize a time when you were in deep stress or distress. What did you learn from whatever was causing you to be repulsed or out of alignment?

....

....

....

....

Take Time to Muse

SHORT SUMMARY: Musing was acknowledged as a powerful way to clearly "see yourself." Taking a purposeful pause, meditation, or going on a personal retreat were listed as helpful tools. All you needed was a special place, time and process.

➡ Do you think the concept of musing is a powerful way to discover your 'A's? Circle what you see as the correct answer:

≈ Absolutely

≈ It's okay, but not sure it's all that great

≈ Puh-lease ; or, "Much ado about nothing"

≈ I'll have to ponder it some more

Hint: the first choice is absolutely the correct answer.

➡ Assuming you'll seriously consider taking time to muse, what can you do on a regular basis that will work best for you?

≈ Prayer

≈ Meditation or Yoga

≈ Personal retreats

≈ Scheduling regular break times

➡ Take a moment to visualize a musing plan for yourself. Complete your thoughts on how you would use these essential ingredients for successful musing:

A Special Place

_____

_____

A Special Time

_____

_____

A Special Process

_____

_____

_____

IMPLEMENTING YOUR 'A'S

Believe That You Can Change

SHORT SUMMARY: We recognized how our belief system determines whether or not we will make positive changes. Knowing that we can change was described as the prerequisite for developing 'A' thoughts and actions.

➡ So, what do you think of the concept of neuroplasticity? Do you agree with the studies stating that your brain can make significant changes regardless of age or previous history? What research presented sounds most compelling to you?

➡ Try this exercise when you experience a negative thought about yourself, following this example:

Example of a negative personal thought: *I'm SO stupid.*

The reframe to neutralize the negative thought: *Sometimes I do things that aren't so smart, but that doesn't make me stupid.*

Your negative thought

Your reframe

➡ Reframing is such an important skill, let's try another exercise that can help.

Describe a *KILLER* 'B' thought or belief that regularly hampers you from doing 'A' activities.

_____

_____

_____

What action can you take to implement your 'A' activity in spite of your *KILLER* 'B' thought or belief?

_____

_____

_____

➡ Since "attitude is everything," you might find the following meditational breathing exercise useful (from *Transforming Anxiety, the HeartMath Solution for Overcoming Fear and Worry and Creating Serenity*, Doc Childre, Deborah Rozman)

Tool: Attitude Breathing

Step 1. Recognize an unwanted attitude: a feeling or attitude that you want to change. This could be overcare, anxiety, self-judgment, guilt, anger, anything.

Step 2. Identify and breathe a replacement attitude: Select a positive attitude, then breathe the feeling of that new attitude slowly and casually through your heart area.

Do this for a while to anchor the new feeling.

Try this several times and report how it works for you.

➡ Write a short essay on the overall attitude you want to have for yourself to insure that you will implement your 'A's.

Start With Your 'A's

SHORT SUMMARY: First Things First was identified as the first commandment for implementing your 'A's. The passion of vision and the power of goals were described as the driving forces behind staying focused on your "main thing."

➡ Visualize one dream idea you have for the next six months. WRITE IT DOWN

_____

_____

_____

➡ Use the S - M - A - R - T goal method to describe how you will implement your vision (see page 108 for review of the method).

S - Specific

_____

M - Measurable

_____

A - Acceptable

_____

R - Realistic

_____

T - Time Frame

_____

➡ The visual for the Pickle Jar theory (not to be confused with the "Pickle theory") was:

enlightening | useful | silly | unnecessary

➡ Maintaining your 'A's is the key to success. How can the image of a **hedgehog** and/or a **flywheel** help your discipline in thought and action? (see page 113)

_____

_____

_____

➡ Choose a "rule" for maintaining your 'A's that makes sense to you. Like the Hedman Rule (page 114), for example! Map out a sample schedule that has you spending 10+ hours a week working on your THRIVING 'A' activities.

Sunday

Monday

Tuesday

Wednesday

Thursday

Friday

Saturday

Total # of hours

Surround Yourself with Other 'A's

SHORT SUMMARY: This chapter emphasized that no one can be a *THRIV-ING* 'A' without help from others. It is imperative to surround yourself with those who "feed you" and to avoid those who "deplete you."

➡ It's difficult to identify those people who are toxic, because they are often family members and/or friends. Nonetheless, acknowledge those people who deplete you. This list should be kept secret; it is just for you.

_____

_____

_____

_____

➡ Describe a situation where you or someone you care about has been a part of a "pity party." What can you do to avoid being a part of these situations?

_____

_____

_____

_____

➡ Think of five people who "feed you" and can help you thrive. Identify them and make them part of your personal 'A' support team.

a)

b)

c)

d)

e)

➡ Identify three - five books (besides this one!) that can inspire and moti-vate you to maintain your 'A's. Keep them close by and refer to them often.

a)

b)

c)

d)

e)

➡ Replicate for yourself Rob's *Feed My 'A' List* method (see page 127). Map out a few weeks.

Week #1 'A' Activities & Goals

Week #2 'A' Activities & Goals

Week #3 'A' Activities & Goals

Find a "Tough Love" Program

SHORT SUMMARY: We stressed how a "tough love" program includes developing a plan and choosing someone (a coach/mentor) to hold you accountable. Finding the right coach was described as a challenging process, but well worth the effort.

➡ First, tough love involves having a plan with a *stretch* goal. Identify three such goals that reflect an 'A' activity.

1) _____

2) _____

3) _____

➡ Second, identify at least three people who will "hold your feet to the fire" in pursuing your goals. They will also hold you accountable by challenging you to move beyond your comfort zone. They could be from the list of people who "feed you," or you may want to choose some others. My three coaches will be:

1) _____

2) _____

3) _____

➡ Since choosing the right coach/mentor team is so difficult, think about the process you will develop to make these choices. List some ideas you have for finding the right match. Define the steps you plan to take.

_____

_____

Be Very Afraid and Have Fun

SHORT SUMMARY: This chapter described the paradox of simultaneously feeling intense fear and enjoyment while attacking KILLER 'B's. Successful strategies included being playful and optimistic, and using laughter and humor.

➡ Try the following strategy outlined by Susan Jeffers in *Feel the Fear and Do It Anyway.*

Describe an 'A' action you are fearful of taking

....

....

Identify the fear

....

....

Ask yourself, *Can I handle the fear? What is the worst that could happen?*

....

....

Ask yourself again, *Can I handle the fear?*

　　Hint: the correct answer is yes.

....

➡ Were you (like millions of other readers) amused by the discussion of Spencer Johnson's *Who Moved My Cheese?* Can you think of ways in which you could be happy about something you find difficult to change? Describe what it might look like:

➡ Closely related to being happy in order to change is the concept of "working hard at play." Describe how playfulness could help you in attacking one of your KILLER 'B's.

➡ From the very personal stories on effectively disarming the 'B's — Dave's Story, Jeff's Story, and the Headmaster's Story (see page 146, 148 and 152) — what do you find applicable to your own story that would help you in implementing your personal 'A's?

Create a Crisis

SHORT SUMMARY: We discussed how implementing your 'A's involves change and crisis, more change and more crisis. Successful decision making was said to occur when your choices are internally generated, conscious and proactive. **Gems** from prose, poetry and quotes were included to further inspire you in taking action.

➡ Practice the *Decision-Making Model for Risk-Takers* for yourself (for a review of the model, see page 156). Outline the following:

Your "stretch goal"

Identify the "wince factor"

Role of your "tough love team"

➡ Recreate for yourself the Psychology class assignment, "Think of something that you fear the most and do it," OR, "Try something you have always wanted to do." Describe what you plan on doing.

➡ For inspirational prose (page 160), **gems** were identified for each of the three authors. Review and describe how you can use these gems.

➡ Poetry (page 163) was presented as a way of "starting a fire in your life." Are you "on fire?!" If so, what in the selected poems did you find inspirational?

➡ Quotes (page 166) - can you believe I included a special quotes section, particularly after you were bombarded with quotes throughout the book? As stated in the text, I find good quotes to be thought-provoking, pungent and memorable. Write down several that will serve as inspirational reminders of how you can successfully implement your 'A's.

➡ This Workbook and Discovery Guide was designed to give you inspiration, ideas and suggestions for becoming a *THRIVING* 'A'. You are encouraged to use any or all of the exercises; try whatever works for you. How would you evaluate the overall effectiveness of this section in helping you reach your goals?

≈ There are many ideas and suggestions that I will use and cherish

≈ I'm "this close" to actively implementing the suggested 'A' habits

≈ The ideas are okay; I'll probably try some in the future

≈ Too much work

≈ Forget about it

This "quiz" is primarily for me to learn what ideas and exercises were useful/not useful, helpful/not helpful for you. I would appreciate your comments on any or all parts of the book. I thank you in advance.

You can reach me through my website: www.dralanhedman.com and don't forget to visit www.killer-b-project.com for more information on living a *THRIVING* life.

REFERENCES / SUGGESTED READINGS

The following recommendations helped form my thinking about what constitutes a THRIVING 'A' life AND how to make it happen. Some were referenced in the book while others were not specifically mentioned, but carry a message you may find valuable.

Feel the Fear and Do It Anyway (1987), Susan Jeffers

Walden (1846), Henry David Thoreau

Flow: The Psychology of Optimal Experience (1990), Mihaly Csikszentmihalyi

What Should I Do with My Life? (2003), Po Bronson

The Death of Ivan Ilych (1886), Leo Tolstoy

Jonathan Livingston Seagull (1970), Richard Bach

The Contrarian's Guide to Leadership (2002), Steven Sample

Living a Life That Matters (2002), Harold Kushner

The 7 Habits of Highly Effective People (1989), Stephen Covey

First Things First (1994), Stephen Covey

The Tyranny of the Urgent (1997), Charles Hummel

The New Testament in Modern English (1962), translated by J. B. Phillips

Your Perfect Right (1975), Robert Alberti

Why Not the Best? (1976), Jimmy Carter

The Four Agreements (1997), Don Miguel Ruiz

The Sweet Spot in Time (1980), John Jerome

Effortless Mastery (1996), Kenny Werner

Cure for the Common Life--Living in Your Sweet Spot (2005), Max Lucado

Celebration of Discipline (1998), Richard J. Foster

Eat, Pray, Love (2006), Elizabeth Gilbert

Train Your Mind, Change Your Brain (2007), Sharon Begley

Good to Great (2001), Jim Collins

The Hedgehog and the Fox (1953), Isaiah Berlin

Outliers (2008), Malcolm Gladwell

Toxic Parents: Overcoming Their Hurtful Legacy and Reclaiming Your Life (2002), Susan Forward

The Secret (2006), Rhonda Byrne

To Begin Again (1999), Naomi Levy

The Road Less Traveled (1978), M. Scott Peck

Who Moved My Cheese?! (1998), Spencer Johnson

Anatomy of an Illness (1979), Norman Cousins

The Language of Emotional Intelligence (2008), Jeanne Segal

Ten Poems to Change Your Life (2001), Roger Housden

About the Author

Meet Dr. Alan Hedman

Alan is a product of his upbringing in the rural setting of Nooksack Valley, WA. He cherishes the values learned there — hard work, persistence, loyalty and responsibility, spiced with a generous dose of story-telling, optimism, and a can-do attitude. Living these values has resulted in some unique successes in a variety of diverse fields including being a champion strawberry picker, an award-winning athlete, and a diligent student who persevered until he earned a Ph.D. in Organizational and Counseling Psychology from the University of Maryland.

Currently, Alan's focus is to help individuals and organizations "learn to thrive." Rather than settling for *business as usual* results, why not work toward personal and professional breakthroughs? And why not reach these goals while enjoying good humor and telling a few stories along the way?

CPSIA information can be obtained at www.ICGtesting.com
Printed in the USA
LVOW120842090312

272330LV00001B/22/P